DATE DUE

ONE HUNDRED YEARS
OF STUDY
ON THE PASSION
NARRATIVES

ONE HUNDRED YEARS
OF STUDY
ON THE PASSION
NARRATIVES

NABPR Bibliographic Series, Number 3

by
David E. Garland

 MERCER UNIVERSITY PRESS, Macon, Georgia 31207

20722613
DLC

5-8-92

ISBN 0-86554-371-2

One Hundred Years of Study
on the Passion Narratives
Copyright © 1989
Mercer University Press

Library of Congress Cataloging-in-Publication Data
Garland, David E.
One hundred years of study
on the Passion narratives / by David E. Garland.
    192 p.   7 x 10—(NABPR bibliographic series; no. 3)
    Includes index
    ISBN 0-86554-371-2 (alk. paper)
    I. Passion narratives (Gospels)—Bibliography.   II. Title.
III. Series.
Z7772.M1G37   1990
[BS2555]
016,226'06—dc20

89-48233
CIP

TABLE OF CONTENTS

EDITOR'S NOTE

This is the third volume to appear in the National Association of Baptist Professors of Religion Bibliographic Series. Other contributions to this series on any aspect of religious or theological studies are invited. Proposals and requests for further information should be sent to: David M. Scholer, NABPR Bibliographic Series Editor, North Park College and Theological Seminary, 3225 West Foster Avenue, Chicago, IL 60625.

NABPR BIBLIOGRAPHIC SERIES

Watson E. Mills
Charismatic Religion in Modern Research:
A Bibliography (1985).

Donald Dean Smeeton
English Religion 1500–1540:
A Bibliography (1988).

PREFACE

It was Martin Kähler (1835–1912) who observed in 1896 that "To state the matter somewhat provocatively, one could call the Gospels passion narratives with extended introductions" (*The So-Called Historical Jesus and the Historic, Biblical Christ,* trans. and ed. Carl E. Braaten [Philadelphia: Fortress, 1964]: 80). In any event, the study of the passion narratives of the Gospels during the last century has been one of the most important aspects of New Testament research.

David E. Garland of Southern Baptist Theological Seminary and a longtime contributor to various aspects of New Testament scholarship provides here a significant bibliography for the continuing investigation of the passion narratives.

David M. Scholer
Chicago, IL
January 1990

ACKNOWLEDGMENTS

This bibliography began in the course of preparing to teach a course on the Passion Narratives in 1977. An attempt has been made to list research over the last hundred years that is directly related to the Passion narrative. It is limited to those works published in English, French, and German. While many bibliographical tools are available today, this one has the advantage of focusing on one particular topic and bringing the wide variety of materials together in one place. It is hoped that this will be useful for any who wish to delve more deeply into the study of the Jesus' Passion.

The bibliography is arranged around the major events of the Passion and includes separate sections on particular topics that have evoked special concern. It is arranged chronologically so that one can more easily trace the development of research and debate. It includes cross references at the end of a section and an author index at the end of the bibliography.

In the course of preparing this bibliography I have made use of the libraries of the Southern Baptist Theological Seminary, Louisville, Kentucky and Eberhard Karls Universität, Tübingen. I am grateful to the staffs of both and to the inter-library loan system. I am also grateful to those in Office Services of SBTS who typed a first draft of the bibliography. I also thank Watson E. Mills of Mercer University Press for his encouragement and cooperation, and particularly Alan Hoskins who provided me with invaluable computer tips that eased the preparation for publication. The bibliography was essentially completed in 1987, but an attempt has been made to include material published in the last year as the bibliography waited to go to press.

—David E. Garland

ABBREVIATIONS

AER	American Ecclesiastical Review
AGJU	Arbeiten zur Geschichte des antiken Judentums und des-Urchristentums
AJT	American Journal of Theology
AnBib	Analecta biblica
AnOr	Analecta orientalia
Anton	Antonianum
AsSeign	Assemblees du Seigneur
ASTI	Annual of the Swedish Theological Institute
ATANT	Abhandlungen zur Theologie des Alten und Neuen Testaments
ATR	Anglican Theological Review
AusBR	Australian Biblical Review
BA	Biblical Archeologist
BARev	Biblical Archaeologist Review
BBB	Bonner biblische Beiträge
BETL	Bibliotheca ephemeridum theologicarum lovaniensium
BEvT	Beiträge zur evangelischen Theologie
BFCT	Beiträge zur Forderung christlicher Theologie
Bib	Biblica
BibB	Biblische Beiträge
BibLeb	Bibel und Leben
BJRL	Bulletin of the John Rylands University Library of Manchester
BK	Bibel und Kirche
BLit	Bibel und Liturgie
BO	Bibliotheca orientalia
BR	Biblical Research
BSac	Bibliotheca Sacra
BT	The Bible Translator
BTB	Biblical Theology Bulletin
BTS	Bible et terre sainte
BVC	Bible et vie chrétienne
BZ	Biblische Zeitschrift

BZAW	Beihefte zur ZAW
BZNW	Beihefte zur ZNW
CBQ	Catholic Biblical Quarterly
CH	Church History
CJT	Canadian Journal of Theology
ClerRev	Clergy Review
ConcJourn	Concordia Journal
ConNT	Coniectanea neotestamentica
CQR	Church Quarterly Review
CTM	Concordia Theological Monthly
CurTM	Currents in Theology and Mission
CV	Communio Viatorum
Down Rev	Downside Review
DunRev	Dunwoodie Review
EBib	Études bibliques
EKKNT	Evangelisch-katholischer Kommentar zum Neuen Testament
EspVie	Esprit et Vie
ETL	Ephemerides theologicae lovanienses
ETR	Études théologiques et religieuses
EvErz	Der evangelische Erzieher
EvQ	Evangelical Quarterly
EvT	Evangelische Theologie
Exp	The Expositor
ExpTim	Expository Times
FB	Forschung zur Bibel
FRLANT	Forschungen zur Religion und Literatur des Alten und Neuen Testaments
FZPT	Freiburger Zeitschrift für Philosophie und Theologie
Greg	Gregorianum
GuL	Geist und Leben
HeyJ	Heythrop Journal
HibJ	Hibbert Journal
HLVG	Das Heilige Land in Vergangenheit und Gegenwart
HTR	Harvard Theological Review
HUCA	Hebrew Union College Annual
IBS	Irish Biblical Studies
IEJ	Israel Exploration Journal
IKZ	Internationale kirchliche Zeitschrift
Int	Interpretation
ITQ	Irish Theological Quarterly

ITS	Indian Theological Studies
JAAR	Journal of the American Academy of Religion
JAMA	Journal of the American Medical Association
JAOS	Journal of the American Oriental Society
JBL	Journal of Biblical Literature
JBR	Journal of Bible and Religion
JEH	Journal of Ecclesiastical History
JES	Journal of Ecumenical Studies
JJS	Journal of Jewish Studies
JNES	Journal of Near East Studies
JQR	Jewish Quarterly Review
JR	Journal of Religion
JRS	Journal of Roman Studies
JSNT	Journal for the Study of the New Testament
JSNTSup	Journal for the Study of the New Testament Supplement Series
JSS	Journal of Semitic Studies
JTS	Journal of Theological Studies
JTS	Africa Journal of Theology for Southern Africa
KD	Kerygma and Dogma
LD	Lectio divina
LingBib	Linguistica Biblica
LMH	Lutherische Monatshefte
LondQR	London Quarterly Review
LQ	Lutheran Quarterly
LS	Louvain Studies
LTS	Lutheran Theological Journal
LumVit	Lumen Vitae
MGWJ	Monatsschrift für Geschichte und Wissenschaft des Judentums
MPT	Monatsschrift für Pastoraltheologie
MTZ	Münchener theologische Zeitschrift
Neot	Neotestamentica
NKZ	Neue kirchliche Zeitschrift
NorTT	Norsk Teologisk Tidsskrift
NovT	Novum Testamentum
NovTSup	Novum Testamentum, Supplements
NRT	La Nouvelle revue théologique
NTAbh	Neutestamentilche Abhandlungen
NTF	Neutestamentliche Forschungen
NTS	New Testament Studies

OBO	Orbis biblicus et orientalis
Or	Orientalia (Rome)
OrBibLov	Orientalia et Biblica Lovaniensa
OTS	Oudtestamentische Studien
PEQ	Palestine Exploration Quarterly
PRS	Perspectives in Religious Studies
PTR	Princeton Tehological Review
QD	Quaestiones Disputae
RA	Revue d'assyriologie et d'archeologie orientale
RArch	Revue archéologique
RB	Revue biblique
RBen	Revue benedictine
REJ	Revue des études juives
RevAT	Revue Africaine de Théologie
RevExp	Review and Expositor
RevQ	Review de Qumran
RevRel	Review for Religious
RevThom	Revue thomiste
RHPR	Revue d'histoire et de philosophie religieuses
RHR	Revue de l'histoire des religions
RSPT	Revue des science philosophiques et théologiques
RSR	Recherches de science religieuse
RTL	Revue théologique de Louvain
RTP	Revue de théologie et de philosophie
SANT	Studien zum Alten und Neuen Testament
SBB	Stuttgarter biblische Beiträge
SBLASP	Society of Biblical Literature Abstracts and Seminar Papers
SBLDS	SBL Dissertation Series
SBS	Stuttgarter Bibelstudien
SBT	Studies in Biblical Theology
ScEs	Science et esprit
Scr	Scripture
SE	Studia Evangelica
SEA	Svensk exegetisk Årsbok
SEAJT	Southeast Asia Journal of Theology
SemioBib	Sémiotique et Bible
SJLA	Studies in Judaism in Late Antiquity
SJT	Scottish Journal of Theology
SNT	Studien zum Neuen Testament
SNTSMS	Society for New Testament Studies Monograph Series

SNTU	Studien zur Umwelt des Neuen Testaments
SO	Symbolae Osloenses
SPB	Studia postbiblica
SR	Studies in Religion/Sciences religieuses
ST	Studia theologica
TBe	Theologische Beiträge
TBl	Theologische Blätter
TBT	The Bible Today
TD	Theology Digest
TF	Theologische Forschung
TGl	Theologie und Glaube
TLZ	Theologische Literaturzeitung
TPQ	Theologisch-Praktische Quartalschrift
TQ	Theologische Quartalschrift
TRu	Theologische Rundschau
TS	Theological Studies
TSK	Theologische Studien und Kritiken
TStudien	Theologische Studien
TTK	Tidsskrift for Teologi og Kirche
TToday	Theology Today
TTZ	Trierer theologische Zeitschrift
TU	Texte und Untersuchungen
TynBul	Tyndale Bulletin
TZ	Theologische Zeitschrift
UNT	Untersuchungen zum Neuen Testament
US	Una Sancta
VC	Vigiliae christianae
VCaro	Verbum caro
VD	Verbum domini
VF	Verkündigung und Forschung
VSpir	Vie spirituelle
VT	Vetus Testamentum
WF	Wege der Forschung
WMANT	Wissenschaftliche Monographien zum Alten and Neuen-Testament
WTJ	Westminster Theological Journal
WUNT	Wissenschaftliche Untersuchungen zum Neuen Testament
WuW	Wissenschaft und Weisheit
WZKM	Wiener Zeitschrift für die kunde des Morgenlandes
ZAW	Zeitschrift für die alttestamentliche Wissenschaft

I. General Treatments of the Passion

Books

0001 Schweitzer, A. *Das Abendmahl — Das Messianitäts und Leidenge-heimnis. Eine Skizze des Lebens Jesu.* 1901. Eng. trans.: *Mystery of the Kingdom of God. The Secret of Jesus' Messiahship and Passion.* Trans. W. Lowrie. London: 1914.

0002 Feigel, F. K. *Der Einfluss des Weissagungsbeweisses und anderer Motive auf die Leidensgeschichte.* Tübingen: 1910.

0003 Belser, J. E. *Die Geschichte des Leidens und Sterbens Jesu.* Freiburg: 1913.

0004 Bertram, G. *Die Leidensgeschichte Jesu und der Christuskult. Eine formgeschichtliche Untersuchung.* FRLANT 32. Göttingen: 1922.

0005 Finegan, J. *Die Überlieferung der Leidens—und Auferstehungs—Geschichte Jesu.* BZNW 15. Giessen: 1934.

0006 Taylor, V. *Jesus and His Sacrifice: A Study of the Passion Sayings in the Gospels.* London: 1937.

0007 Hillmann, W. *Aufbau und Deutung der synoptischen-Leidensberichte. Ein Beitrag zur Kompositionstechnik und-Sinndeutung der drei älteren Evangelien.* 1941.

0008 Bornhäuser, K. *Die Leidens— und Auferstehungsgeschichte Jesu.* Gütersloh: 1947. Eng. trans.: *The Death and Resurrection of Christ.* Trans. A. Rumpus. London: 1958.

0009 Innitzer, T. *Kommentar zur Leidens— und Verklärungsgeschichte Christ.* 4. Aufl. Vienna: 1948.

0010 Schelkle, K. H. *Die Passion Jesu in der Verkündigung des Neuen Testaments: Ein Beitrag zur Formgeschichte und zur Theologie des Neuen Testaments*. Heidelberg: 1949.

0011 Bornkamm, G. *Jesus von Nazareth*. 2 Aufl. Stuttgart: 1957, 141-154. = *Jesus of Nazareth*. Trans. I. and F. McLuskey and J. M. Robinson. New York: 1960, 153-168.

0012 Bultmann, R. *Die Geschichte der synoptischen Tradition*. 3 Aufl. FRLANT 12. Göttingen: 1957, 282-308. Eng. Trans.: *History of the Synoptic Tradition*. Trans. J. Marsh. Oxford: 1963, 262-284.

0013 Taylor, V. *The Cross of Christ*. London: 1957.

0014 Knox, J. *The Death of Christ: The Cross in New Testament History and Faith*. New York: 1958.

0015 Dibelius, M. *Die Formgeschichte des Evangeliums*. 3 Aufl. Tübingen: 1959, 178-219. Eng. Trans.: *From Tradition to Gospel*. Trans. B. L. Woolf. New York: 178-217.

0016 Hooker, M. D. *Jesus and the Servant: The Influence of the Servant Concept of Deutero-Isaiah in the New Testament*. London: 1959.

0017 Wyon, O. *The Grace of the Passion*. London: 1959.

0018 Barclay, W. *Crucified and Crowned*. London: 1960.

0019 Kohler, M. *Artisans et partisans de la Croix*. Neuchatel: 1961.

0020 Lohse, E. *Die Geschichte des Leidens und Sterbens Jesu Christi*. Gütersloh: 1964. Eng. Trans.: *History and Suffering and Death of Jesus Christ*. Trans. O. Dietrich. Philadelphia: 1967.

0021 Benoit, P. *Passion et Résurrection du Seigneur*. Paris: 1966. Eng. trans.: *The Passion and Resurrection of Jesus Christ*. Trans. B. Weatherhead. New York: 1969.

0022 Barrett, C. K. *History and Faith: The Story of the Passion*. London: 1967.

0023 Popkes, W. *Christus Traditus. Eine Untersuchung zum Begriff der Dahingabe im Neue Testament*. ATANT 49. Zurich: 1967.

0024 Linnemann, E. *Studien zur Passionsgeschichte*. FRLANT 102. Göttingen: 1970.

0025 Martinez, E. R. *The Gospel Accounts of the Death of Jesus*. Rome: 1970.

0026 Wilson, W. R. *The Execution of Jesus: A Judicial, Literary and Historical Investigation*. New York: 1970.

0027 Delling, G. *Der Kreuzestod Jesu in der unchristlichen Verkündigung*. Berlin: 1971.

0028 Guillet, J. *Jésus devant sa vie et sa mort*. Paris: 1971.

0029 Marin, L. *Semiotique de la Passion. Topiques et figures*. Paris: 1971. Eng. trans: *The Semiotics of the Passion Narrative*. Trans. A. M. Johnson. PTMS 25. Pittsburgh: 1980.

0030 Ruppert, L. *Jesus als der leidende Gerechte?* SBS 59. Stuttgart: 1972.

0031 Bednarz, M. *Les éléments parénétiques dans la description de la Passion chez les synoptiques*. Rome: 1973.

0032 Schneider, G. *Die Passion Jesu nach den drei alteren Evangelien*. Munich: 1973.

0033 Schenke, L. *Der gekreuzigte Christus*. SBS 69. Stuttgart: 1974.

0034 Schürmann, H. *Jesu ureigener Tod. Exegetische Besinnungen und Ausblick*. Freiburg: 1975.

0035 Williams, S. K. *Jesus' Death as Saving Event*. HDR 2. Missoula: 1975.

0036 Gollwitzer, H. *Jesu Tod und Auferstehung*. 6th ed. Munich: 1976.

0037 Kertelge, K. (ed.). *Der Tod Jesu. Deutungen im Neuen Testament*. QD 74. Freiburg/Basel/Vienna: 1976.

0038 Gubler, M. L. *Die frühesten Deutungen des Todes Jesu*. OBO 15. Freiburg/Göttingen: 1977.

0039 Weber, H. R. *Kreuz: Überlieferung und Deutung der Kreuzigung Jesu im Neutestamentlichen Kulturraum*. Stuttgart: 1975. Eng. trans.: *The Cross: Tradition and Interpretation*. Trans. E. Jessett. Grand Rapids: 1979.

0040 Hendrickx, H. *The Passion Narratives of the Synoptic Gospels*. Manila: 1978.

0041 Murphy, R. T. A. *Days of Glory. The Passion, Death and Resurrection of Jesus Christ*. Ann Arbor, MI: 1980.

0042 Steichele, H. J. *Der leidende Sohn Gottes*. BU 14. Regensburg: 1980.

0043 Zehrer, F. *Das Leiden Christi nach den vier Evangelien: Die wichtigsten Passionstexte und ihre hauptsachlichen Probleme*. Vienna: 1980.

0044 Limbeck, M. (ed.). *Redaktion und Theologie des Passionsberichtes nach den Synoptikern*. WF 481. Darmstadt: 1981.

0045 Lohfink, G. *Der letzte Tag Jesu. Die Ereignisseder Passion*. Freiburg/ Basel/ Vienna: 1981. Eng. trans.: *The Last Day of Jesus:*

A Enriching Portrayal of the Passion. Trans. S. Attanasio. Notre Dame: 1984.

0046 Flusser, D. *Die letzten Tage Jesu in Jerusalem. Das Passionsgeschehen aus jüdischer Sicht. Bericht über neueste Forschungsergebnisse.* Trans. H. Zechner. Stuttgart: 1982.

0047 Friedrich, G. *Die Verkündigung des Todes Jesu im Neuen Testament.* BTS 6. Neukirchen/Vluyn: 1982.

0048 White, R. E. O. *The Night He Was Betrayed. Bible Studies in Our Lord's Preparation for His Passion.* Grand Rapids: 1982.

0049 Leenhardt, F. J. *La mort et le testament de Jésus.* Essais bibliques 6. Geneva: 1983.

0050 Trocme, E. *The Passion as Liturgy. A Study in the Origin of the Passion Narratives in the Four Gospels.* London: 1983.

0051 Bammel, E. and Moule, C. F. D. (ed.) *Jesus and the Politics of His Day.* Cambridge: 1984.

0052 Boinnard, Y. *Mort de Jésus. Dossier pour l'animation biblique.* Essais bibliques 8. Geneva: 1984.

0053 Kleinknecht, K. T. *Der leidende Gerechtfertigte. Die alttestamentlich— jüdische Tradition vom ''leidende Gerechten'' und ihre Rezeption bei Paulus.* WUNT 2/13. Tübingen: 1984.

0054 Allison, D. C. *The End of the Ages Has Come. An Early Interpretation of the Passion Resurrection of Jesus.* Philadelphia: 1985.

0055 Schweitzer, A. *The Mystery of the Kingdom of God. The Secret of Jesus' Messiahship and Passion.* Trans. W. Lowrie. Buffalo: 1985.

0056 Kelly, J. N. D. *Aspects of the Passion.* London: 1985.

0057 Zwanzger, W. *Christus für uns gestorben. Die evangelische Passions Predigt.* Stuttgart: 1985.

0058 Brown, R. E. *A Crucified Christ in Holy Week. Essays on the Four Gospel Passion Narratives.* Collegeville, MN: 1986.

0059 Matera, F. J. *Passion Narratives and Gospel Theologies.* New York: 1986.

0060 Navone, J. and Cooper, T. *The Story of the Passion.* Rome: 1986.

0061 Stott, J. R. W. *The Cross of Christ.* Downers Grove: 1986.

0062 Grassi, J. A. *Rediscovering the Impact of Jesus' Death.* Kansas City: 1987.

Articles

0063 Zingerle, C. P. "Über und aus Reden von Zwei syrischen Kirchenvätern über das Leiden Jesu," *TQ* 52 (1870) 92-114; 53 (1871) 409-426.

0064 Simonsen, D. "Le Psaume XXII et la Passion de Jésus," *RJ* 22 (1891) 283-285.

0065 Carr, A. "Hostile and Alien Evidence for Christ at Passiontide," *Exp* 6th ser. 7 (1903) 417-425.

0066 Howland, S. H. "The Reason and Nature of Christ's Sufferings," *BSac* 62 (1905) 514-537.

0067 Pfättisch, J. M. "Christus und Sokrates bei Justin," *TQ* 90 (1908) 503-523.

0068 Haggard, A. M. "Problems of the Passion Week," *BSac* 69 (1912) 664-692.

0069 Holzmeister, U. "Die Passionsliteratur der letzten sechs Jahre (1909-1914). Eine Übersicht über die Behandlung der Hauptfragen aus dem Leiden Christi," *ZKT* 39 (1915) 318-367.

0070 Bostick, W. F. "Jesus and Socrates," *BW* 47 (1916) 248-252.

0071 Moffatt, J. "Jesus as Prisoner," *ExpT* 28 (1916-17) 57-62.

0072 Buchanan, E. S. "New Light on the Passion of our Lord Jesus Christ," *BibSac* 74 (1917) 610-613.

0073 Moffatt, J. "Jesus and the Four Men," *ExpT* 32 (1920-21) 486-489.

0074 Schmidt, K. L. "Die literarische Eigenart der Leidengeschichte," *Die Christliche Welt* 32 (1918) 114-116.

0075 Belden, A. D. "The Spirit of Expiation," *RevExp* 22 (1925) 228-233.

0076 Dibelius, M. "Das historische Problem der Leidengeschichte," *ZNW* 30 (1931) 193-201. *Botschaft und Geschichte*. Tübingen: 1953, 248-257.

0077 Dibelius, M. "La signification religieuse de récits évangéliques de la Passion," *RHPR* 13 (1933) 30-45.

0078 Bleiben, T. E. "The Synoptists Interpretation of the Death of Christ," *ExpT* 54 (1942-43) 145-149.

0079 Fascher, E. "Sokrates und Christus," *ZNW* 45 (1945) 1-41.

0080 Bishop, E. F. F. "With Jesus on the Road from Galilee to Calvary: Palestinian Glimpses into the Days Around the Passion," *CBQ* 11 (1949) 428-444.

0081 Michl, J. "Der Tod Jesu. Ein Beitrag zur Frage nach Schuld und Verantwortung eines Volkes," *MTZ* 1 (1950) 5-15.

0082 Benz, E. "Christus und Sokrates in der alten Kirche," *ZNW* 43 (1950-51) 195-224.

0083 Hope, C. "The Story of the Passion and Resurrection in the English Primer," *JTS* 2 (1951) 68-82

0084 Léon-Dufour, X. "Mt et Mc dans le récit de las Passion," *Bib* 40 (1959) 684-696.

0085 Schmid, J. "Die Darstellung der Passion Jesu in den Evangelien," *GuL* 27 (1954) 6-15.

0086 Schille, G. "Das Leiden des Herrn. Die evangelische Passionstradition und ihr 'Sitz im Leben'," *ZTK* 52 (1955) 161-205.

0087 Davies, P. E. "Did Jesus die as a Martyr-Prophet?" *BR* 2 (1957) 19-30.

0088 Leenhardt, F. J. "Réflexions sur la mort de Jésus-Christ," *RHPR* 37 (1957) 18-23.

0089 Schnackenburg, R. "Vom Aergernis des Kreuzes," *GuL* 30 (1957) 90-95.

0090 Whiteley, D. E. H. "Christ's Foreknowledge of His Crucifixion," *SE* I (TU 73 1959) 100-114.

0091 Léon-Dufour, X. "Autour des récits de la Passion," *RSR* 48 (1960) 489-507.

0092 Bruce, F. F. "The Book of Zechariah and the Passion Narrative," *BJRL* 43 (1960-61) 342-345.

0093 Isaac, J. "Problèmes de la Passion d'aprés deux études récentes," *Revue Historique* 85 (1961) 119-138.

0094 Marxsen, W. "Erwägungen zum Problem der Verkündigten Kreuzes," *NTS* 8 (1961-1962) 204-214.

0095 Ballentine, G. L. "Death of Jesus as the New Exodus," *RevExp* 59 (1962) 27-41.

0096 Bartsch, H. W. "Historische Erwägungen zur Leidensgeschichte," *ErT* 22 (1962) 449-459.

0097 Finegan, J. "A Quest for the History Behind the Passion," *JBT* 16 (1962) 102-104.

0098 Rose, A. "L'influence des psaumes sur les annonces et les récits de la Passion et de la Résurrection dans les Évangiles," *OrBibLov* 4 (1962) 297-356.

0099 Downing, J. "Jesus and Martyrdom," *JTS* 14 (1963) 279-293.

0100 Bartsch, H. W. "Die Bedeutung des Sterbens Jesu nach den Synoptikern," *TZ* 20 (1964) 87-102.

0101 Hruby, H. "Das Leiden des Messias," *Jud*20 (1964) 193-212.

0102 Ramsey, A. M. "The Narratives of the Passion," *SE* II (TU 87 1964) 122-134.

0103 Bligh, J. "Typology in the Passion Narratives: Daniel, Elijah, Melchizedek," *HeyJ* 6 (1965) 302-309.

0104 Seils, M. "Zur Frage nach der Heilsbedeutung des Kreuzestodes Jesu," *TLZ* 90 (1965) 881-894.

0105 Summers, R. "The Death and Resurrection of Jesus," *RevExp* 62 (1965) 473-481.

0106 Trilling, W. "Die Passionsgeschichte in den synoptischen Evangelien," *Lebendiges Zeugnis* 1 (1966) 28-46.

0107 Boris, L. "Das Kreuz des Menschsein,"*Orientierung* 21 (1967) 56-59.

0108 Conzelmann, H. "Historie und Theologie in den synoptischen Passionsberichten," *Zur Bedeutung des todes Jesu.* Ed. F. Viering. Gütersloh: 1967, 35-53. Eng. Trans.: "History and Theology in the Passion Narratives of the Synoptic Gospels," *Int* 24 (1970) 178-197.

0109 Schrage, W. "Das Verständnis des Todes Jesus Christi im Neuen Testament," *Das Kreuz Jesu Christi als Grund des Heils.* Gütersloh: 1967.

0110 Vanhoye, A. "Structure et théologie des récits de la Passion dans les évangiles synoptiques," *NRT* 89 (1967) 135-163. Eng. trans.: *Structure and Theology of the Accounts of the Passion in the Synoptic Gospels.* Trans. C. H. Giblin. Collegeville: 1967.

0111 Dodd, C. H. "The Historical Problem of the Death of Jesus," *More New Testament Studies.* Grand Rapids: 1968, 84-101.

0112 Feuillet, A. "Les trois grandes prophéties de la Passion et de la Résurrection des évangiles synoptiques," *RevThom* 68 (1968) 41-74.

0113 Flessemann van Leer, E. "Die Interpretation der Passionsgeschichte vom AT aus," *Zur Bedeutung des Todes Jesu.* Ed. F. Viering. Gütersloh: 1968, 79-96.

0114 Käsemann, E. "Historie und Theologie in den synoptischen Passionsberichten," *Zur Bedeutung des Todes Jesu.* Ed. F. Viering. Gütersloh: 1968, 35-53.

0115 Kreck, W. "Zum Verständnis des Todes Jesu," *EvT* 28 (1968) 277-293.

0116 Lohse, E. "Die alttestamentliche Bezüge im neutestamentlichen Zeugnis vom Tode Jesu Christi," *Zur Bedeutung des Todes Jesu.* Ed. F. Viering. Gütersloh: 1968, 97-112.

0117 Riedl, J. "Die Evangelische Leidensgeschichte und ihre theologische Aussage," *BLit* 41 (1968) 70-111.

0118 Roi, J. "Simples réflexions sur la Passion de Notre-Seigneur," *BVC* 81 (1968) 58-65.

0119 Black, M. "The 'Son of Man' Passion Sayings in the Gospel Tradition," *ZNW* 60 (1969) 1-8.

0120 Davies, A. T. "The Jews and the Death of Jesus," *Int* 23 (1969) 207-217.

0121 Brandenburger, E. "*Stauros,* Kreuzigung Jesu and Kreuzestheologie," *Wort und Dienst* 10 (1969) 17-43.

0122 Coune, M. "Baptême, Transfiguration, Passion,"*Foi et Vie* 7 (1969) 38-55.

0123 Strobel, A. "Die Deutung des Todes Jesu in ältesten Evangelium," *Das Kreuz Jesu.* Ed. P. Rieger. Göttingen: 1969, 32-64.

0124 Wilson, R. McL. "The New *Passion of Jesus* in the Light of the New Testament and Apocrypha," *Neotestamentica et Semitica.* Ed. E. E. Ellis and M. Wilcox (Fest. M. Black). Edinburgh: 1969, 264-271.

0125 Chevallier, M. A. "La prédication de la croix," *ETR* 45 (1970) 131-161.

0126 Coune, M. "Baptême, Transfiguration, et Passion," *NRT* 92 (1970) 165-179.

0127 Perrin, N. "The Use of (*para*) *didonai* in Connection with the Passion of Jesus in the New Testament," *Der Ruf Jesu und die Antwort der Gemeinde.* Ed. E. Lohse (Fest. J. Jeremias). Göttingen: 1970, 204-212.

0128 Richardson, P. "The Israel-Idea in the Passion Narratives," *The Trial of Jesus.* Ed. E. Bammel. SBT 2d. ser. 13. Naperville, IL.: 1970, 1-10.

0129 Chabrol, C. "Analyse des 'Textes' der Passion," *Langages* 22 (1971). = *Erzählende Semiotik nach Berichten der Bibel.* Ed. C. Chabrol. Munich: 1973, 123-155.

0130 Crespy, G. "Recherche sur le signification politique de la mort du Christ," *Lumière et Vie* 20 (1971) 89-109.

0131 Duquoc, C. "Théologie brève de la mort du Christ," *Lumière et Vie* 20 (1971) 110-121.

0132 George, A. "Comment Jésus a-t-il percu sa propre mort?" *Lumière et Vie* 20 (1971) 34-59.

0133 Paul, A. "Pluralité des interpretations théologiques de la mort due Christ dans le Nouveau Testament," *Lumière et Vie* 20 (1971) 18-33.

0134 Suggs, M. J. "The Passion and Resurrection Narratives," *Jesus and Man's Hope*. Ed. D. G. Miller. Pittsburgh: 1971, 323-338.

0135 Vanhoye, A. "Les récits de la Passion dans les évangiles synoptiques," *AsSeign* 19 (1971) 38-67.

0136 Horbury, W. "The Passion Narratives and Historical Criticism," *Theology* 75 (1972) 58-71.

0137 Lange, H. D. "The Relationship between Psalm 22 and the Passion Narrative," *CTM* 43 (1972) 610-621.

0138 Roloff, J. "Anfange der soteriologischen Deutung des Todes Jesu (Mk. x.45 und Lk. xxii.27)," *NTS* 19 (1972-73) 38-64.

0139 Janssen, F. "Die synoptischen Passionsberichte. Ihre theologische Konzeption und literarische Komposition," *BibLeb* 14 (1973) 40-57.

0140 Schürmann, H. "Wie hat Jesus seinem Tod bestanden und verstanden?" *Orientierung an Jesus*. Ed. P. Hoffmann, N. Brox and W. Pesch (Fest. J. Schmid). Freiburg: 1973, 325-363.

0141 Zehrer, F. "Sinn und Problematic der Schriftverwendung in der Passion," *TPQ* 121 (1973) 18-25.

0142 Davies, P. E. "Did Jesus Die as a Martyr-Prophet," *BR* 19 (1974) 37-47.

0143 Guillet, J. "Les récits de la Passion," *Lumière et Vie* 23 (1974) 6-17.

0144 Kertelge, K. "Der allgemeine Tod und der Tod Jesu," *TTZ* 83 (1974) 146-156.

0145 Luz, U. "Theologia Crucis als Mitte der Theologie im Neuen Testament," *EvT* 34 (1974) 116-141.

0146 O'Donovan, L. J. "Approaches to the Passion," *Worship* 48 (1974) 130-142.

0147 Pesch, R. "Die Überlieferung der Passion Jesu," *Rückfrage nach Jesus*. Ed. K. Kertelge. Freiburg: 1974, 148-173.

0148 Pesch, R. "Zur Theologie des Todes Jesu. Ein Versuch," *Kontinuität in Jesus. Zugange zu Leben, Tod und Auferstehung*. Ed. R. Pesch and A. H. Zwergel. Freiburg: 1974, 73-94.

0149 Zehrer, F. "Jesus, der leidende Gerechte, in der Passion," *BLit* 47 (1974) 104-111.

0150 Kuhn, H. W. "Jesus als Gekreuzigter in der früchristlichen Verkündigung bis zur Mitte des 2. Jahrhunderts," *ZTK* 72 (1975) 1-46.

0151 de Jonge, M. "The Use of *ho christos* in the Passion Narratives," *Jésus aux origines de la christologie.* Ed. J. Dupont. BETL 40. Gembloux: 1975, 169-192.

0152 Schwank, B. "Das Verständnis des Todes Jesu in Neuen Testament," *Erbe und Auftrag* 51 (1975) 237-240.

0153 Lindars, B. "The Apocalyptic Myth and the Death of Christ," *BJRL* 57 (1975) 366-387.

0154 Czerski, J. "Die Passion Christi in den synoptischen Evangelien im Lichte der historisch-literarischen Kritik," *Collectanea Theologica* 46 (1976) 81-96.

0155 Donahue, J. R. "Introduction: From Passion Traditions to Passion Narrative," *The Passion in Mark: Studies on Mark 14:16.* Ed. W. H. Kelber. Philadelphia: 1976, 1-20.

0156 Gnilka, J. "Wie urteilte Jesus über seinen Tod?" *Der Tod Jesu. Deutungen im Neuen Testament.* Ed. K. Kertelge. QD 74. Freiburg: 1976, 13-50.

0157 Kelber, W. H. "Conclusion: From Passion Narrative to Gospel," *The Passion in Mark: Studies on Mark 14-16.* Ed. W. H. Kelber, Philadelphia: 1976, 153-180.

0158 Léon-Dufour, X. "Jesus' Understanding of His Death," *TD* 24 (1976) 293-300.

0159 O'Collins, G. "The Crucifixion," *Doctrine and Life* 26 (1976) 247-263.

0160 Evans, C. F. "The Tradition of the Passion," *Exploration in Theology 2.* London: 1977, 3-17.

0161 Evans, C. F. "The Event of the Passion," *Exploration in Theology 2.* London: 1977, 18-33.

0162 Flusser, D. "The Crucified One and the Jews," *Immanuel* 7 (1977) 25-37.

0163 Pathrapankal, J. "The Cross of Jesus," *Jeevadhara* 7 (1977) 213-221.

0164 Kretschmar, G. "Kreuz und Auferstehung Jesu Christi. Das Zeugnis der Heiligen Stätten," *Erbe und Auftrag* 54 (1978) 423-431.

0165 Schneider, G. "Die theologische Sicht des Todes Jesu in den Kreuzigungsberichten der Evangelien," *TPQ* 126 (1978) 14-22.

0166 Wrege, H. T. "Die Passionsgeschichte," *Die Gestalt des Evangeliums*. BET 11. Frankfurt/Bern/Las Vegas: 1978, 49-96.

0167 Oswald, J. "Die Beziehungen zwischen Psalm 22 und dem vormarkinischen Passionsbericht," *ZKT* 101 (1979) 53-66.

0168 Schillebeeckx, E. "Section Two: Kingdom of God, rejection and death of Jesus," *Jesus: An Experiment in Christology*. Trans. H. Hoskins. New York: 1979, 272-319.

0169 Cousin, H. "Dieu a-t-il sacrifié son fils Jésus?" *LumVit* 29 (1980) 55-67.

0170 Hengel, M. "The Expiatory Sacrifice of Christ," *BJRL* 62 (1980) 454-475.

0171 Galvin, J. P. "Jesus' Approach to Death: An Examination of Some Recent Studies," *TS* 41 (1980) 713-749.

0172 Kümmel, W. G. "Jesusforschung seit 1965. Der Prozess und der Kreuzestod Jesu," *TRu* 45 (1980) 293-337.

0173 Schürmann, H. "Jesu Todesverständnis Verstehenshorizont seiner Umwelt," *TGl* 70 (1980) 141-158. = *Gottes Reich— Jesu Geschick*. Freiburg/Basel/Vienna: 1983, 225-245.

0174 Schürmann, H. "Jesu ureigenes Todesverständnis: Bemerkungen zur 'implizierten Soteriologie' Jesu," *Begegnung mit dem Wort*. Ed. J. Zmijewski and E. Nellessen. BBB 53. Bonn: 1980: 272-309. = *Gottes Reich—Jesu Geschick*. Freiburg/Basel/Vienna: 1983, 185-223.

0175 Harrington, W. "Passion and Death," *Doctrine and Life* 31 (1981) 136-142.

0176 Léon-Dufour, X. "How Did Jesus See His Death?" *TD* 29 (1981) 57-60.

0177 McCaffrey, U. P. "Psalm quotations in the passion narratives of the Gospels," *Neot* 14 (1981) 73-89.

0178 O'Neill, J. C. "Did Jesus Teach that His Death Would be Vicarious as well as Typical?" *Suffering and Martyrdom in the New Testament*. Ed. W. Horbury and B. McNeill. Cambridge: 1981, 9-27.

0179 Cambe, M. "Le récits de la Passion en relation avec différents textes du IIe siècle," *Foi et Vie* 81 (1982) 12-24.

0180 Stadelmann, L. I. J. "The Passion Narrative in the Synoptics as Structured on Ps 22 (21)," *Perspectiva Teologica* 15 (1983) 193-221.

0181 Derrett, J. D. M. "Daniel and Salvation History," *Downside Review* 100 (1982) 63-68. = *Studies in the New Testament*. Leiden: 1986, 132-138.

0182 Radl, W. "Der Tod Jesu in der Darstellung der Evangelien," *TGl* 72 (1982) 432-446.

0183 Watty, W. W. "Jesus and the Temple—Cleansing or Cursing?" *ExpT* 93 (1982) 235-239.

0184 Biser, E. "Die älteste Passionsgeschichte," *GuL* 56 (1983) 111-118.

0185 Marshall, I. H. "The Death of Jesus in Recent New Testament Study," *Word and World* 3 (1983) 12-21.

0186 Kurichianil, J. "Jesus' Consciousness of His Passion and Death According to the Synoptic Gospels," *Bible Bhashyam* 9 (1983) 114-125.

0187 Saxer, V. "Le 'Juste Crucifié' de Platon à Theoderet," *Rivista di Storia e Letteratura Religiosa* 19 (1983) 189-215.

0188 Leroy, M. V. "Mort et Résurrection," *RevThom* 84 (1984) 261-291.

0189 Schenk, W. "Der derzeigte Stand der Auslegung der Passionsgeschichte," *Der Evangelische Erzieher* 36 (1984) 527-543.

0190 Viennas, D. "The Passion History as Holy War," *Direction* 13 (1984) 26-32.

0191 Aletti, J. N. "Mort de Jésus et théorie du récit," *RSR* 73 (1985) 147-160.

0192 Beauchamp, P. "Narrativite biblique du récit de la Passion," *RSR* 73 (1985) 39-59.

0193 Calloud, J. "Entre les écritures et la violence. La passion du temoin," *RSR* 73 (1985) 111-128.

0194 Delorme, J. "Sémiotique du récit et récit de la passion," *RSR* 73 (1985) 85-109.

0195 Grappe, C. "Essai sur l'arrière-plan pascal des récits de la derniere nuit de Jésus," *RHPR* 65 (1985) 105-125.

0196 Haulotte, E. "Du récit quadriforme de la Passion au concept de Croix," *RSR* 73 (1985) 187-228.

0197 Mays, J. L. "Prayer and Christology: Psalm 22 as Perspective on the Passion," *ThToday* 42 (1985) 322-331.

0198 Ricoeur, P. "Le récit interpretaif. Exègése et Théologie dans le récits de la Passion," *RSR* 73 (1985) 17-38.

0199 Schaberg, J. "Daniel 7,12 and the New Testament Passion-Resurrection Predictions," *NTS* 31 (1985) 208-222.

0200 Scholz, G. " 'Joseph von Arimathäa' und 'Barabbas'. Beobachtungen zur narrativen Ausgestaltung der Auslieferungs— und der
Stellvertretungstheologie," *LingBib* 57 (1985) 81-94.

0201 Schwager, R. "Christ's and the Prophetic Critique of Sacrifice," *Semeia* 33 (1985) 109-123.

0202 Stuhlmacher, P. "Warum musste Jesus sterben?" *TBe* 16 (1985) 273-
285.

0203 Watson, F. "Why was Jesus Crucified?" *Theology* 88 (1985) 105-
112.

0204 Merklein, H. "Der Tod Jesu als stellervertretender Suhnetod. Entwicklung und Gehalt einer zentraler neutestamentlichen Aussage," *BK* 41 (1986) 68-75.

0205 Schwager, R. "Der Tod Christi und die Opferkritik," *Theologie der
Gegenwart* 29 (1986) 11-20.

0206 Weiser, A. "Der Tod Jesu und das Heil der Menschen. Aussagew-
eisen von Erlösung im Neuen Testament," *BK* 41 (1986) 60-67.

0207 Borg, M. J. "The Jesus Seminar and the Passion Sayings," *Forum*
3 (1987) 81-95.

0208 Butts, J. R. "Passion Apologetic, the Chreia, and the Narrative,"
Forum 3 (1987) 96-127.

0209 Dillon, R. J. "The Psalms of the Suffering Just In the Accounts of
Jesus' Passion," *Worship* 61 (1987) 430-440.

0210 Girard, R. "The Gospel Passion as Victim's Story," *Cross Currents*
36 (1986-87) 28-38.

0211 Skoog, A. "The Jews, the Church and the Passion of Christ," *Immanuel* 21 (1987) 236-240.

0212 Moberly, W. "Proclaiming Christ Crucified: Some Reflections on
the Use and Abuse of the Gospels," *Anvil* 5 (1988) 31-52.

II. The Passion
and Source Criticism

Books

0213 Perry, A. M. *The Sources of Luke's Passion Narrative*. Chicago: 1919.

0214 Taylor, V. *Behind the Third Gospel: A Study of the Proto-Luke Hypothesis*. Oxford: 1926.

0215 Rehkopf, F. *Die lukanische Sonderquelle. Ihr Umfang und Sprachgebrauch*. WUNT 5. Tübingen: 1957.

0216 Green, J. B. *The Death of Jesus. Tradition and Interpretation in the Passion Narrative*. WUNT 2/33 Tübingen: 1988.

Articles

0217 Hawkins, J. C. "St. Luke's Passion Narrative considered with reference to the Synoptic Problem," *ExpT* 15 (1903-04) 122-126, 273-276.

0218 Buckley, E. R. "The Sources of the Passion Narrative in St. Mark's Gospel," *JTS* 34 (1932-33) 138-144.

0219 Perry, A. M. "Some Outstanding New Testament Problems, V. Luke's Disputed Passion-Source," *ExpT* 46 (1934-35) 256-260.

0220 Creed, J. M. "The Supposed 'Proto-Lucan' Narrative of the Trial before Pilate: A Rejoinder," *ExpT* 46 (1934-35) 378-379.

0221 Hanson, R. P. C. "Does *dikaios* in Luke 23:47 Explode the Proto-Luke Hypothesis," *Hermathena* 60 (1942) 74-78.

0222 Barr, A. "The Use and Disposal of the Marcan Source in Luke's Passion Narrative," *ExpT* 55 (1943-44) 227-231.

0223 Taylor, V. "The Origin of the Markan Passion Sayings," *NTS* 1 (1954-55) 159-169 = *New Testament Essays*. London: 1972, 59-76.

0224 Taylor, V. "Sources of the Lukan Passion Narrative," *ExpT* 68 (1956-57) 95.

0225 Winter, P. "Sources of the Lucan Passion Narrative," *ExpT* 68 (1956-57) 95.

0226 Buse, S. J. "St. John and the Marcan Passion Narrative," *NTS* 4 (1957-58) 215-219.

0227 Schneider, G. "Das Problem einer vorkanischen Passionserzählung," *BZ* 16 (1972) 222-244.

0228 Cribbs, L. "A Study of the Contacts that Exist Between St. Luke and St. John," SBLASP (1973) 2: 46-81.

0229 Smith, D. M. "The Setting and Shape of a Johannine Narrative Source," *JBL* 95 (1976) 231-241.

0230 Fortna, R. T. "Jesus and Peter are the High Priest's House: A Test Case for the Question of the Relation Between Mark's and John's Gospels," *NTS* 24 (1978) 371-382.

0231 Soards, M. L. "The Question of a Pre-Markan Passion Narrative," *Bible Bhashyam* 11 (1985) 144-169.

0232 White, J. L. "The Way of the Cross: Was There a Pre-Markan Passion Narrative?" *Forum* 3 (1987) 35-49.

See also 0167, 0314, 0319, 0344, 0354, 0356, 0360, 0387, 0393, 0411, 0415, 1355, 1394

III. The Passion of Matthew

Books

0233 Fascher, E. *Das Weib des Pilatus (Matthäus 27,19). Die Auferweckung der Heiligen (Matthäus 27,51-53).* Halle: 1951.

0234 Kratz, R. *Auferweckung als Befreiung. Eine Studie zur Passions-und Auferstehungstheologie des Matthäus. (Besonders Mt. 27,62-28:15).* SBS 65. Stuttgart: 1973.

0235 Senior, D. P. *The Passion Narrative according to Matthew. A Redactional Study.* BETL 39. Leuven: 1975.

0236 Riebl, M. *Auferstehung Jesu in der Stunde seines Todes? Zur Botschaft von Mt 27,51b-53.* Stuttgart: 1978.

0237 Senior, D. P. *The Passion of Jesus in the Gospel of Matthew.* Wilmington, 1985.

0238 Houlden, J. L. *Backward into Light: The Passion and Resurrection of Jesus According to Matthew and Mark.* London: 1987.

0239 Thurston, B. B. *Wait Here and Watch: A Commentary on the Passion According to Saint Matthew.* St Louis, 1989.

Articles

0240 Sparks, H. "St. Matthew's Reference to Jeremiah," *JTS* 1 (1950) 155-156.

0241 Dahl, N. A. "Die Passionsgeschichte bei Matthäus," *NTS* 2 (1955) 17-32. Eng. Trans.: "The Passion Narrative in Matthew," *Jesus in the Memory of the Early Church.* Minneapolis: 1976, 37-51.

0242 Baumstark, A. "Die Zitate des Mt.-Evangeliums aus dem Zwölfprophetenbuch," *Biblica* 37 (1956) 296-313.

0243 Bartsch, H. W. "Die Passions-und Ostergeschichten bei Matthäus. Ein Beitrag zur Redaktionsgeschichte des Evangeliums," *Entmythologisierende und Auslegung*. TF 26. Hamburg: 1962, 80-92.

0244 Trilling, W. "Der Passionsbericht nach Matthäus," *Am Tisch des Wortes* 3 (1965) 33-44,

0245 Bligh, J. "Matching Passages, 2: St. Matthew's Passion Narrative," *Way* 9 (1969) 59-73.

0246 Gerhardsson, B. "Jésus livré et abandonné d'après la Passion selon saint Matthieu," *RB* 76 (1969) 206-227.

0247 Fischer, K. M. "Redaktionsgeschichtliche Bermerkungen zur Passionsgeschichte des Matthäus,"*Theologische Versuche*. Berlin: 1970, 2:109-129.

0248 Quinn, J. F. "The Pilate Sequence in the Gospel of Matthew," *DunRev* 10, 1970 154-177.

0249 Descamps, A. "Rédaction et christologie dans le récit matthéen de la Passion," *L'Évangile selon Matthieu*. Ed. M. Didier, BETL 29. Gembloux: 1972, 359-416.

0250 Senior, D. P. "The Passion Narrative in the Gospel of Matthew," *L'évangile selon Matthieu*. Ed. M. Didier. BETL 29. Gembloux: 1972, 343-357.

0251 Lai, P. H. "Production du sens par la foi. Autorités religieuses contestées/fondées. Analyse structurale de Matthieu 27,57-28,20," *RSR* 61 (1973)65-96.

0252 Senior, D. P. "The Death of Jesus and the Resurrection of the Holy Ones (Mt. 27:51-53)," *CBQ* 38 (1976) 312-329.

0253 Punnakottil, G. "The Passion Narrative According to Matthew. A Redaction Critical Study," *Bible Bhashyam* 3 (1977) 20-47.

0254 Escande, J. "Judas et Pilate prisonniers d'une même structure (Mt. 27,1-26), *Foi et Vie* 18 (1979) 92-100.

0255 Rieckert, S. J. P. K. "The Narrative Coherence in Matthew 26-28," *Structure and Meaning in Matthew 14-28*. Neotestamentica 16. 1982, 53-74.

0256 Brown, R. E. "The Passion According to Matthew," *Worship* 58 (1984) 98-107.

0257 Matera, F. J.. "Matthew 27:11-54," *Int* 38 (1984) 55-59.

0258 Hill, D. "Matthew 27:51-53 in the Theology of the Evangelist," *IBS* 7 (1985) 76-87.

0259 Turiot, C. "Sémiotique et lisibilité du texte évangélique," *RSR* 73 (1985) 161-175.

0260 Buck, E. "Anti-Judaic Sentiments in the Passion Narrative According to Matthew," *Anti-Judaism in Early Christianity: Volume 1. Paul and the Gospels*. Ed. P. Richardson and D. Granskou. Waterloo, Ont.: 1986, 165-180.

0261 Lodge, J. G. "Matthew's Passion—Resurrection Narrative," *Chicago Studies* 25 (1986) 3-20.

0262 LaVerdiere, E. A. "The Passion Story as Prophecy," *Emmanuel* 93 (1987) 85-90.

0263 Martin, F. and Panier, L. "Devoilement du peche et salut dans le récit de la passion selon saint Matthieu," *Lumière et Vie* 36 (1987) 72-88.

0264 Matera, F. J. "The Passion According to Matthew. Part One: Jesus Unleashes the Passion, 26:1-75," *ClerRev* 62 (1987) 93-97.

0265 Matera, F. J. "The Passion According to Matthew. Part Two: Jesus Suffers the Passion, 27:1-66," *Priests & People* 1 (1987) 13-17.

0266 Senior, D. P. "Matthew's Special Material in the Passion Story: Implications for the Evangelist's Redactional Technique and Theological Perspective," *ETL* 63 (1987) 272-294.

See also 0303, 0419, 0736, 0849, 0853, 0861, 0878, 0887,0887, 0895, 0926, 0998, 1027, 1133, 1135, 1137, 1158, 1162, 1166, 1184, 1191, 1500-1529, 1581, 1613, 1625, 1637, 1638, 1659, 1690, 1699-1711, 1854-1900, 1904, 1915, 1941, 1965, 2003-2014, 2027, 2049, 2052, 2053

IV. The Passion of Mark

Books

0267 Schreiber, J. *Die Markuspassion: Wege zur Erforschung der Lei-densgeschichte*. Hamburg: 1969.

0268 Chordat, J. L. *Jésus, devant sa mort dans l'Évangile de Marc*. Paris: 1970.

0269 Schenke, L. *Studien zur Passionsgeschichte des Markus. Tradition und Redaktion in Markus 14:1-42*. Würzburg: 1971.

0270 Best, E. *The Temptation and the Passion: The Markan Soteriology*. SNTS 2. Cambridge: 1965.

0271 Van Ruler, A. A. *Marcus 14,1-41*. Kampen: 1971.

0272 Donahue, J. R. *"Are You the Christ?" The Trial Narrative in the Gospel of Mark*. SBLDS 10. Missoula: 1973.

0273 Dormeyer, D. *Die Passion Jesu als Verhaltensmodell. Literarische und theologishe Analyse der Traditions— und Redaktionsges-chichte der Markus Passion*. NTAbh 11. Münster: 1974.

0274 Schenk, W. *Der Passionsbericht nach Markus*. Berlin: 1974.

0275 Schenke, L. *Der gekreuzigte Christus. Versuch einer literarkri-tischen und traditionsgeschichtlichen Bestimmung der vormar-kinischen Passionsgeschichte*. SBS 69. Stuttgart: 1974.

0276 Schlier, H. *Die Markuspassion*. Einsiedeln: 1974.

0277 Kelber, W. H. ed. *The Passion in Mark: Studies on Mark 14-16*. Philadelphia: 1976.

0278 Juel, D. *Messiah and Temple: The Trial of Jesus in the Gospel of Mark*. SBLDS 31. Missoula, Mont.: 1977.

0279 Genest, O. *Le Christ de la Passion Perspective Structurale. Analyse de Marc 14,53-15,47 des parallèles bibliques et extra-bibliques*. RT 21. Montreal: 1978.

0280 Patte, D. and Patte, A.. *Structural Exegesis: From Theory to Prac-tice. Exegesis of Mark 15 and 16. Hermeneutical Implications.* Philadelphia: 1978.

0281 Dormeyer, D. *Der Sinn des Leidens Jesu. Historisch-kritische und textpragmatische Analysen zur Markuspassion.* SBS 96. Stutt-gart: 1979.

0282 Pesch, R. *Das Evangelium der Urgemeinde.* Freiburg: 1979.

0283 Mann, D. *Mein Gott, mein Gott, warum hast du mich verlassen? Auslegung der Passionsgeschichte nach Markus.* Neukirchen/Vluyn: 1980.

0284 Matera, F. J. *The Kingship of Jesus. Composition and Theology in Mark 15.* SBLDS 66. Chico, Cal.: 1982.

0285 Mohr, T. A. *Markus— und Johannespassion. Redaktions— und traditionsgeschichtliche Untersuchung der markinischen und jo-hanneischen Passionstradition.* ATANT 70. Zurich: 1982.

0286 Rosaz, M. and Pousset, E.. *Passion-Resurrection. Selon l'évangile de saint Marc.* Supplement à Vie Chrétienne 276. Paris: 1984.

0287 Senior, D. P. *The Passion of Jesus in the Gospel of Mark.* Wilming-ton: 1984.

0288 Blackwell, J. *The Passion as Story: The Plot of Mark.* Philadelphia: 1986.

0289 Navone, J. and Cooper, T.. *The Story of the Passion.* Rome: 1986.

0290 Schreiber, J. *Der Kreuzigungsbericht des Markusevangeliums: Mk 15,20b-41. Eine traditionsgeschichtliche und methodenkritische Untersuchung nach William Wrede (1859-1906).* BZNWKAK 48. Berlin/NewYork: 1986.

0291 Houlden, J. L. *Backward into Light: The Passion and Resurrection of Jesus According to Matthew and Mark.* London: 1987.

0292 Ruhland, M. *Die Markuspassion aus der Sicht der Verleugnung.* Eil-brunn: 1987.

Articles

0293 Riddle, D. W. "The Martyr Motif in the Gospel According to Mark," *JR* 4 (1924) 397-410.

0294 Buckley, E. R. "The Sources of the Passion Narrative in St. Mark's Gospel," *JTS* 34 (1933) 138-144.

0295 Kiddle, M. "The Death of Jesus and the Admission of the Gentiles in St. Mark," *JTS* 35 (1934) 45-50.

0296 Lightfoot, R. H. "IV. The Connexion of Chapter Thirteen with the Passion Narrative," *The Gospel Message of St. Mark*. Oxford: 1950 48-59.

0297 Grayston, K. "The Darkness of the Cosmic Sea: A Study of Symbolism in Mark's Narrative of the Crucifixion," *Theology* 55 (1952) 122-127.

0298 Maurer, C. "Knecht Gottes und Sohn Gottes im Passionsbericht des Markusevangeliums," *ZTK* 50 (1953) 1-38.

0299 Taylor, V. "The Origin of the Markan Passion-Sayings," *NTS* 1 (1954-55) 159-167.

0300 Piper, O. A. "God's Good News: The Passion Story According to Mark," *Int* 9 (1955) 165-182.

0301 Cowling, C. C. "Mark's Use of *hōra*," *AusBR* 5 (1956) 154-160.

0302 Burkill, T. A. "St. Mark's Philosophy of the Passion," *NovT* 2 (1958) 245-271.

0303 Léon-Dufour, X. "Mt et Mc dans le récit de la Passion," *Bib* 40 (1959) 684-696.

0304 Léon-Dufour, X. "Mt et Mc dans le récit de la Passion," *Studia Biblica et Orientlia*. Rome: 1959, 2:116-128.

0305 Dewar, F. "Chapter 13 and the Passion Narrative in St. Mark," *Th* 64 (1961) 99-107.

0306 Tyson, J. B. "The Blindness of the Disciples in Mark," *JBL* 80 (1961) 261-268.

0307 Suhl, A. "Die alttestamentlichen Zitate in der Leidensgeschichte des Markusevangeliums," *Die Funktion der alttestamentlichen Zitate und Anspielungen in der Leidensgeschichte des Markusevangeliums*. Gütersloh: 1965, 26-66.

0308 Danker, F. W. "The Literary Unity of Mark 14:1-25," *JBL* 85 (1966) 467-472

0309 Strecker, G. "Die Leidens— und Auferstehungsvoraussagen im Markusevangelium," *ZTK* 64 (1967) 16-39. Eng. Trans. "The Passion and Resurrection Predictions in Mark's Gospel (Mark 8:31; 9:13; 10:32-34)," *Int* 22 (1968) 421-442.

0310 Schenk, W. "Die gnostisierende Deutung des Todes Jesu und ihre kritische Interpretation durch den Evangelisten Markus," *Gnosis und Neues Testament*. Ed. K. W. Tröger. Gütersloh: 1973, 231-243.

0311 Smith, R. H. "Darkness at Noon: Mark's Passion Narrative," *CTM* 44 (1973) 325-338.

0312 Bartsch, H. W. "Der ursprüngliche Schluss der Leidengeschichte. Überlieferungsgeschichtliche Studien zum Markus—Schluss," *L'Évangile selon Marc. Tradition et rédaction*. Ed. M. Sabbe, BETL 34. Leuven/Gembloux: 1974, 411-433.

0313 Mourlon Beernaert, P. "Structure littéraire et lecture théologique de Marc 14,17-52" *L'Évangile Selon Marc. Tradition et rédaction* Ed. M. Sabbe. BETL 34. Leuven/Gembloux: 1974, 241-267.

0314 Pesch, R. "Der Schluss der vormarkinischen Passionsgeschichte und des Markusevangeliums: Mk. 15,42-16,8," *L'évangile selon Marc*. BETL 34. Leuven/Gembloux: 1974, 435-470.

0315 Schüngel, P. H. "Die Erzählung des Markus über den Tod Jesu," *Orientierung* 38 (1974) 62-65.

0316 Burkill, T. A. "Blasphemy: St. Mark's Gospel as Damnation History," *Christianity, Judaism and Other Greco-Roman Cults*. Ed. J. Neusner. Leiden: Brill, 1975, I: 51-74.

0317 Kee, H. C. "The Function of Scriptural Quotations and Allusions in Mark 11-16," *Jesus and Paulus*. Ed. E. E. Ellis and E. Grässer (Fest. W. G. Kümmel). Göttingen: 1975, 165-188.

0318 Juel, D. "The Function of the Trial of Jesus in Mark's Gospel," SBLASP (1975) 2: 83-104.

0319 Pesch, R. "Die Passion des Menschensohnes. Eine Studie zu den Menschensohnworten der vormarkinischen Passionsgeschichte," *Jesus und der Menschensohn*. Ed. R. Pesch and R. Schnackenburg (Fest. A. Vögtle). Freiburg: 1975, 166-195.

0320 Schenk, W. "Die gnostisierende Deutung des Todes Jesu und ihre kritische Interpretation durch den Evangelisten Markus," *Gnosis und Neues Testament*. Berlin: 1975, 231-243.

0321 Culpepper, R. A. "The Passion and Resurrection in Mark," *RevExp* 75, (1978) 583-600.

0322 Oswald, J. "Die Beziehungen zwischen Psalm 22 und dem vormarkinishen Passionsbericht," *ZKT* 101 (1979) 53-66.

0323 Zeller, D. "Die Handlungsstruktur der Markuspassion. Der Ertrag strukturalistischer Literaturwissenschaft für die Exegese," *TQ* 159 (1979) 213-227.

0324 Ernst, J. "Die Passionserzählung des Markus und die Aporien den Forschung," *TGl* 70 (1980) 160-180.

0325 O'Grady, J. F. "The Passion in Mark," *BTB* 10 (1980) 83-87.

0326 Meyer, R. P. "Die Botschaft der Leidensgeschichte Jesus Christi nach Markus. Bibelarbeit in Gruppen," *BK* 36 (1981) 246-249.

0327 Smith, M. "The Composition of Mark 11-16," *HJ* 22 (1981) 363-377.

0328 Veerkemp, T. "Vom ersten Tag nach jenem Sabbat. Der Epilog des Markusevangeliums: 15,33-16,8," *Texte & Kontexte* 13 (1982) 5-34.

0329 Wiéner, C. "Le mystère pascal dans le deuxième évangile. Recherches sur la construction de Marc 14-16," *La Pâque di Christi, Mystère de salut. Mélanges offerts au P.F.-X. Durrwell pour son 70e anniversaire*. Paris: 1982, 131-145.

0330 Riches, J. "The Passion According to Mark—Divine Power and Suffering," *The New Testament as Personal Reading*. Ed. R. Drury. Springfield, IL. 1983, 118-130.

0331 Stanley, D. M. "Mark's Passion—Narrative. Four proleptic symbolic acts (10,46-11,25)," *Way* supp. 46 (1983) 67-77.

0332 Vellanickal, M. "The Passion Narrative in the Gospel of Mark (Mk. 14:1-15:47)," *Bible Bhashyam* 9 (1983) 258-278.

0333 Brown, R. E. "The Passion according to Mark," *Worship* 59 (1985) 116-126.

0334 Lull, D. J. "Interpreting Mark's Story of Jesus' Death: Toward a Theology of Suffering," *SBLASP* (1985) 1-12.

0335 Navone, J. "Mark's Story of the Death of Jesus," *New Blackfriars* 65 (1985) 123-135.

0336 Anderson, C. P. "The Trial of Jesus as Jewish-Christian Polarization: Blasphemy and Polemic in Mark's Gospel," *Anti-Judaism in Early Christianity: Volume 1. Paul and the Gospels*. Ed. P. Richardson and D. Granskou. Waterloo, Ont.: 1986, 107-126.

0337 Senior, D. P. "Crucible of Truth: Passion and Resurrection in the Gospel of Mark," *Chicago Studies* 25 (1986) 21-34.

0338 Johnson, E. S. "Is Mark 15.39 the Key to Mark's Christology?" *JSNT* 31 (1987) 3-22.

0339 Lee-Pollard, D. A. "Powerlessness as Power: A Key Emphasis in the Gospel of Mark," *SJT* 40 (1987) 173-188.

0340 Watson, F. "Ambiguity in the Markan Narrative," *King's Theological Review* 10 (1987) 11-16.

0340a McVann, M. "The Passion in Mark: Transformation Ritual," *BTB* 18 (1988) 96-101.

0341 Navone, J. ''The Last Day and the Last Supper in Mark's Gospel,''
   Theology 91 (1988) 38-43.

0342 Oberlinner,L. ''Die Botschaft vom Kreuz als die Botschaft vom Heil
   nach Markus,'' *BLit* 61 (1988) 56-65.

   See also 0218, 0223, 0226, 0227, 0230, 0231, 0232, 0414, 0729,
   0737, 0749, 0780, 0789, 0791, 0809, 0891, 0896, 0901, 0905,
   0907, 0912, 0926, 0929, 0933, 0937, 0947, 0948, 0951, 0960,
   0962, 0997, 1000, 1044, 1046, 1088, 1134, 1144, 1146, 1151,
   1168, 1170, 1177, 1178, 1181, 1183, 1186, 1187, 1371, 1386,
   1398, 1404, 1477, 1479, 1499, 1787, 1797, 1799, 1800, 1804,
   1806, 1808, 1809, 1810, 1813, 1819, 1821, 1829, 1854-1900,
   1904, 1942, 1945, 1952, 1956, 1961, 1964, 1967, 1970, 1974,
   1975, 1976, 2038, 2050, 2054, 2109

V. The Passion of Luke

Books

0343 Gollwitzer, H. *Jesu Tod und Auferstehung nach dem Bericht des Lukas.* Munich: 1951.

0344 Vööbus, A. *The Prelude to the Lukan Passion Narrative: Tradition—, Redaction—, Cult—, Motif—historical and Source Critical Studies.* Papers of the Estonian Theological Society in Exile. Stockholm: 1968.

0345 Brown, S. *Apostasy and Perserverence in the Theology of Luke.* AnBib 36. Rome: 1969.

0346 Schneider, G. *Verleugnung, Verspottung und Verhör Jesu nach Lukas 22:54-71. Studien zur lukanischen Darstellung der Passion.* SANT 22. Munich: 1969.

0347 Taylor, V. *"The Passion Narrative of St. Luke: A Critical and Historical Investigation.* SNTSMS 19. Cambridge: 1972.

0348 Buchele, A. *Der Tod Jesu im Lukas-evangelium. Eine Redaktionsgeschichtliche Untersuchung zu Lk. 23.* FTS 26. Frankfurt: 1978.

0349 Bösen, W. *Jesusmahl. Eucharistisches Mahl. Endzeitsmahl. Ein Beitrag zur Theologie des Lukas.* SB 97. Stuttgart: 1980.

0350 Untergassmair, F. G. *Kreuzweg und Kreuzigung Jesu. Ein Beitrag zur lukanischen Redaktionsgeschichte und zur Frage nach der lukanischen Kreuzestheologie (Lc 23,26-49).* PTS 10. Paderborn: 1980.

0351 Karris, R. J. *Luke: Artist and Theologian: Luke's Passion Account as Literature.* New York/Mahwah: 1985.

0352 Neyrey, J. H. *The Passion According to Luke: A Redaction Study of Luke's Soteriology.* New York/Mahwah: 1985.

0353 Tyson, J. B. *The Death of Jesus in Luke-Acts.* Columbia, S.C.: 1986.

0354 Soards, M. L. *The Passion According to Luke: The Special Material of Luke 22.* JSNTS 14. Sheffield: 1987.

0355 Senior , D. *The Passion in the Gospel of Luke.* Wilmington: 1989.

Articles

0356 Perry, A. M. "Luke's Disputed Passion—Source," *ExpT* 46 (1934-35) 255-260.

0357 Kiddle, M. "The Passion Narrative in St. Luke's Gospel," *JTS* 36 (1935) 267-280.

0358 Kilpatrick, G. D. "A Theme of the Lucan Passion Story and Luke XXIII.47," *JTS* 43 (1942) 34-36.

0359 Osty, E. "Les points de contact entre le récit de la Passion dans saint Luc et saint Jean," *RSR* 39 (1951-52) 146-154.

0360 Winter, P. "The Treatment of His Sources by the Third Evangelist in Luke XXI-XXIV," *ST* 8 (1954-55) 138-172.

0361 Winter, P. "Luke XXII.66b-71," *ST* 9 (1955-56) 112-115.

0362 Tyson, J. B. "The Lukan Version of the Trial of Jesus," *NovT* 3 (1959) 249-258.

0363 Stalder, K. "Die Heilsbedeutung des Todes Jesu in den lukanischen Schriften," *Internationale Kirchliche Zeitschrift* 52 (1962) 222-242.

0364 Rau, G. "Das Volk in der lukanischen Passionsgeschichte, eine Konjektur zu LC 23,13," *ZNW* 56 (1965) 41-51.

0365 Blevins, J. L. "The Passion Narrative," *RevExp* 64 (1967) 513-522.

0366 Blinzler, J. "Passionsgeschehen und Passionsbericht des Lukas-evangeliums," *BK* 24 (1969) 1-4.

0367 Stöger, A. "Eigenart und Botschaft der lukanischen Passionsge-schichte," *BK* 24 (1969) 4-8.

0368 Zehnle, R. "The Salvific Character of Jesus' Death in Lucan Sote-riology," *TS* 30 (1969) 420-444.

0369 Grosch, H. " 'Andere hat er gerettet . . .' Exegetische und didak-tische Besinnung über zwei lukanische Passionstexte," *EvErz* 22 (1970) 233-247.

0370 Vööbus, A. "Kritische Beobachtungen über die lukanische Darstel-lung des Herrenmahls," *ZNW* 61 (1970) 102-109.

0371 George, A. "Le sens de la mort de Jésus pour Luc," *RB* 80 (1973) 186-217.

0372 Trilling, W. "Le Christ, roi crucifié (Lc 23)," *AsSeign* 65 (1973) 56-67.

0373 Klein, H. "Die lukanisch— johanneische Passionstradition," *ZNW* 67 (1976) 155-186.

0374 Smith, R. H. "Paradise Today: Luke's Passion Narrative," *CurTM* 3 (1976) 323-336.

0375 Crowe, J. "The *LAOS* at the Cross: Luke's Crucifixion Scene," *The Language of the Cross*. Ed. A. Lacomara. Chicago: 1977, 79-90.

0376 Larkin, W. J. "Luke's Use of the Old Testament as a Key to His Soteriology," *JETS* 20 (1977) 325-335.

0377 Smalley, W. A. "Translating Luke's Passion Story from the *TEV*," *BT* 28 (1977) 231-235.

0378 Kodell, J. "Luke's Theology of the Death of Jesus," *Sin, Salvation and the Spirit*. Ed. D. Durken. Collegeville, Mn: 1979, 221-230.

0379 Untergassmair, F. G. "Thesen zur Sinndeutung des Todes Jesu in der lukanischen Passiongeschichte," *TGl* 70 (1980) 180-193.

0380 Beck, B. E. " 'Imitatio Christi' and the Lucan Passion Narrative," *Suffering and Matyrdom in the New Testament*. Ed. W. Horbury and B. McNeil. Cambridge: 1981, 28-47.

0381 Monsarrat, V. "Le récit de la Passion: un enseignement pour le disciple fidèle. Luc 22-23," *FoiVie* 81 (1982) 40-47.

0382 Jankowski, G. "Passah und Passion. Die Einleitung der Passiongeschichte bei Lukas," *Texte & Kontexte* 13 (1982) 40-60.

0383 Cassidy, R. J. "Luke's Audience, the Chief Priests and the Motive for Jesus' Death," *Political Issues in Luke-Acts*. Ed. R. J. Cassidy and P. J. Scharper. Maryknoll: 1983, 146-167.

0384 LaVerdiere, E. A. "The Eucharist in Luke's Gospel," *Emmanuel* 89 (1983) 446-449, 452-453.

0385 Schmidt, D. "Luke's 'Innocent' Jesus: A Scriptural Apologetic," *Political Issues in Luke-Acts*. Ed. R. J. Cassidy and P. J. Scharper. Maryknoll: 1983, 111-121.

0386 Via, E. J. "According to Luke, Who Put Jesus to Death?" *Political Issues in Luke-Acts*. Ed. R. J. Cassidy and P.J. Scharper. Maryknoll: 1983, 122-145.

0387 Matera, F. J. "The Death of Jesus according to Luke: A Question of Sources," *CBQ* 47 (1985) 469-485.

0388 Brown, R. E. "The Passion According to Luke," *Worship* 60 (1986) 2-9.

0389 Gaston, L. "Anti-Judaism and the Passion Narrative in Luke and Acts," *Anti-Judaism in Early Christianity: Volume 1. Paul and the Gospels.* Ed. P. Richardson and D. Granskou. Waterloo, Ont.: 1986, 127-153.

0390 Kany, R. "Der lukanische Bericht von Tod und Auferstehung Jesu aus der Sicht eines hellenistischen Romanlesers," *NovT* 28 (1986) 75-90.

0391 LaVerdiere, E. A. "The Passion-Resurrection of Jesus according to St. Luke," *Chicago Studies* 25 (1986) 35-50.

0392 Ravens, D. A. S. "St Luke and Atonement," *ExpT* 97 (1986) 291-294.

See also 0214, 0215, 0217, 0219, 0220, 0221, 0222, 0224, 0225, 0228, 0411, 0419, 0438, 0695, 0696, 0697, 0706, 0721, 0722, 0727, 0728, 0730, 0734, 0736, 0739, 0747, 0759, 0760, 0762, 0764, 0765, 0771, 0772, 0777, 0779, 0782, 0785, 0791, 0792, 0793, 0795, 0796, 0810, 0818, 0820, 0826, 0840, 0849, 0870, 0879, 0880, 0883, 0904, 0918, 0922, 0939, 0949, 0941, 0946, 0950, 0952, 0953, 0954, 0957, 0959, 0964, 0969, 0971, 0974, 0975, 0976-0990, 1019, 1094, 1294, 1409, 1410, 1446, 1463, 1497, 1651, 1664-1683, 1751, 1754, 1757, 1758, 1759, 1765, 1768, 1777, 1778, 1782, 1786, 1789, 1792, 1793, 1818, 1820, 1822, 1826, 1827, 1828, 1830-1853, 1908, 1918, 1928, 1930, 1938, 1950, 1972, 2025

VI. The Passion of John

Books

0393 Goguel, M. *Les sources du récit johannique de la Passion*. Paris: 1910.

0394 Geyer, M. *Die Johannespassion*. Bad Pyrmont: 1941.

0395 Fenton, J. C. *The Passion According to John*. London: 1961.

0396 Freed, E. D. *Old Testament Quotations in the Gospel of John*. NovTSup 11. Leiden: 1965.

0397 Meeks, W. A. *The Prophet-King: Moses Traditions and the Christology*. NovTSup 14. Leiden: 1967.

0398 Dauer, A. *Die Passionsgeschichte im Johannesevangelium: Eine traditionsgeschichtliche und theologische Untersuchung zu Joh. 18,1-19,30*. SANT 30. Munich: 1972.

0399 Leistner, R. *Antijudäismus im Johannesevangelium? Darstellung des Problems in der neueren Auslegungsgeschichte und Untersuchung der Leidensgeschichte*. Bern/Frankfurt: 1974.

0400 Pancaro, S. *The Law in the Fourth Gospel*. NovTSup 42. Leiden: 1975.

0401 Vanhoye, A., de la Potterie, I., Duquoc, C. and Charpentier, E. (eds.). *La passion selon les quartre Évangiles*. Paris: 1981.

0402 Nicholson, G. C. *Death as Departure. The Johannine Descent-Ascent Schema* SBLDS 63. Chico, CA: 1983.

0403 Baum-Bodenbender, R. *Hoheit in Niedrigkeit. Johanneische Christologie im Prozess Jesu vor Pilatus (Joh 18,28-19,16a)*. FB 49. Würzburg: 1984.

0404 de la Potterie, I. *La passion de Jésus selon l'évangile de Jean. Texte et Esprit*. Lire la Bible 73. Paris: 1986.

0405 Panackel, C. *IDOY OH ANTHRŌPOS(Jn 19,5b). An Exegetico-Theological Study of the Text in the Light of the Use of the Term ANTHRŌPOS Designating Jesus in the Fourth Gospel.* AG 251. Rome: 1988.

Articles

0406 Askwith, E. H. "The Historical Value of the Fourth Gospel. IV. The Trial of Jesus," *Exp* 7th ser. 8 (1909) 431-441.

0407 Askwith, E. H. "The Historical Value of the Fourth Gospel. V. The Crucifixion," *Exp* 7th ser. 8 (1909) 520-542.

0408 Dibelius, M. "Die altestamentlichen Motive in der Leidensgeschichte des Petrus— und des Johannes— Evangeliums," *BZAW* 33 (1917) 125-150 = *Botschaft und Geschichte*. Tübingen: 1953, 1:221-247.

0409 Church, W. B. "The Dislocations in the 18th Chapter of John," *JBL* 49 (1930) 375, 383.

0410 Braun, F. M. "La Passion de Notre-Seigneur Jésus-Christ selon Saint Jean," *NRT* 60 (1933), 289-302; 385-400; 481-499.

0411 Osty, E. "Les points de contact entre le récit de la passion dans saint Luc et dans saint Jean," *RSR* 39 (1951) 146-154.

0412 Dodd, C. H. "The Passion Narrative," *The Interpretation of the Fourth Gospel*. Cambridge: 1953, 423-443.

0413 Schneider, J. "Zur Komposition von Joh 18,12-27. Kaiphas und Hannas," *ZNW* 48 (1957) 111-119.

0414 Buse, I. "St. John and the Marcan Passion Narrative," *NTS* 4 (1957-58) 215-218.

0415 Borgen, P. "John and the Synoptics in the Passion Narrative," *NTS* 5 (1958-59) 246-259.

0416 Ziener, G. "Johannesevangelium und urchristliche Passafeier," *BZ* 2 (1958) 263-274.

0417 Stanley, D. M. "The Passion according to St. John," *Worship* 33 (1958-59) 210-230.

0418 Blank, J. "Die Verhandlung vor Pilatus. Jo 18,28-19,16 im Lichte johanneischer Theologie," *BZ* 3 (1959) 60-81.

0419 Buse, I. "St. John & the Passion Narratives of St. Matthew and St. Luke," *NTS* 7 (1959-60) 65-76.

0420 de la Potterie, I. "Jésus roi et juge d'après Jn 19,13 *ekathisen epi bēmatos*," *Bib* 41 (1960) 217-247. Eng. trans.: "Jesus King and Judge according to John xix.13," *Scr* 13 (1961) 97-111.

0421 Haenchen, E. "Jesus vor Pilatus (Joh. 18,28-19,15)," *TLZ* 80 (1960), 93-102.

0422 Janssens de Varebeke, A. "La structure des scènes du récit de la passion en Joh. XVIII-XIX," *ETL* 38 (1962) 504-522.

0423 Dodd, C. H. "The Passion Narrative," *Historical Tradition in the Fourth Gospel.* Cambridge: 1965, 21-151.

0424 Riaud, J. "La gloire et la royauté de Jésus dans la passion selon saint Jean," *BVC* 56 (1964) 28-44.

0425 Schelkle, K. H. "Die Leidensgeschichte Jesu nach Johannes. Motiv- und formgeschichtliche Betrachtung," *Am Tisch des Wortes 2* (1965) 43-49. = *Wort und Schrift.* Düsseldorf: 1966, 76-80.

0426 Summers, R. "The Death and Resurrection of Jesus: John 18-21," *RevExp* 62 (1965) 473-481.

0427 Weise, M. "Passionswoche und Epiphaniewoche im Johannes— Evangelium. Ihre Bedeutung für Komposition und Konzeption des vierten Evangeliums," *KD* 12 (1966) 48-62.

0428 Haenchen, E. "Historie und Geschichte in den johanneischen Pas- sionsberichten," *Zur Bedeutung des Todes Jesu.* Ed. F. Viering. Gütersloh: 1967, 55-78. Eng. trans.: "History and Interpretation in the Passion Narrative," *Int* 24 (1970) 198-219.

0429 Howard, J. K. "Passover and Eucharist in the Fourth Gospel," *SJT* 20 (1967) 329-337.

0430 Richter, G. "Die Deutung des Kreuzestodes Jesu in der Leidensges- chichte des Johannesevangelium (Jo 13-19)," *Bib Leb* 9 (1968) 21-36. = *Studien zum Johannesevangelium.* Regensburg: 1977, 58-73.

0431 de la Potterie, I. "La Passion selon saint Jean (Jn 18,1-19, 42)," *AsSeign* 21 (1969) 21-34.

0432 Hahn, F. "Der Prozess Jesu nach dem Johannesevangelium," *EKKNT* 2. Zurich/Neukirchen: 1970, 23-96.

0433 White, R. E. O. "Christ's Death as John Saw It," *Christianity To- day* 16 (1972) 548-551.

0434 Boismard, C. "La royauté universelle du Christ (Jn 18)," *AsSeign* 65 (1973) 36-47.

0435 Mollat, D. "La foi pascale selon le chapitre 20 de l'Évangile de saint Jean. Essai de théologie biblique," *Resurrexit. Actes du symposium international sur la Résurrection de Jésus*. Rome: 1974, 316-339.

0436 Brown, R. E. "The Passion According to John: Chapters 18 and 19," *Worship* 49 (1975) 126-134.

0437 Müller, U. B. "Die Bedeutung des Kreuzestodes Jesu im Johannesevangelium," *KD* 21 (1975) 49-71.

0438 Klein, H. "Die lukanisch— johanneische Passionstradition," *ZNW* 67 (1976) 155-186.

0439 Lindars, B. "The Passion in the Fourth Gospel," *God's Christ and His People*. Ed. G. W. E. Nickelsburg and G. W. MacRae (Fest. N. Dahl). Oslo: 1976, 71-84.

0440 Pfitzner, V. C. "The Coronation of the King—Passion Narrative and Passion Theology in the Gospel of St. John," *LTJ* 10 (1976) 1-12.

0441 Baumeister, T. "Der Tod Jesu und die Leidensnachfolge des Jüngers nach dem Johannesevangelium um dem Ersten Johannesbrief," *WuW* 40 (1977) 81-99.

0442 Lacomara, A. "The Death of Jesus as Revelation in John's Gospel," *The Language of the Passion*. Ed. A. Lacomara. Chicago: 1977, 103-127.

0443 Beutler, J. "Psalm 42/43 im Johannesevangelium," *NTS* 25 (1978) 33-57.

0444 Giesen, H. "Die Passionsgeschichte nach Joh 18,1-19,42," *Am Tisch des Wortes* 164 (1978) 55-71. = *Glaube und Handeln*. Frankfort/Bern/New York: 1983, 161-172.

0445 Morgan-Wynne, J. E. "The Cross and the Revelation of Jesus as *ego eimi* in the Fourth Gospel (John 8:28)," *SB* 2 (JSNTSS 2, 1980) 219-226.

0446 Sproston, W. E. "Satan in the Fourth Gospel," *SB* 2 (JSNTSS 2, 1980) 307-311.

0447 de la Potterie, I. "La mort du Christ d'après Saint Jean," *Studia Missionala* 31 (1982) 19-36.

0448 L'Eplattenier, C. "La Passion dans l'évangile de Jean," *Foi et Vie* 81 (1982) 25-30.

0449 McHugh, J. "The Glory of the Cross: The Passion According to St. John," *ClerRev* 67 (1982) 117-127.

0450 Borgen, P. "John and the Synoptics in the Passion Narrative," *Logos Was the True Light*. Trondheim: 1983, 67-80.

0451 Giesen, H. "Die Stunde Jesu. Die Passionsgeschichte nach Joh 18,1-19,42," *Beiträge zur Exegese und Theologie des Neuen Testaments*. Frankfurt/Bern/New York: 1983, 2:161-172.

0452 Hengel, M. "Reich Christi, Reich Gottes und Weltreich im 4. Evangelium," *TBe* 14 (1983) 201-216.

0453 Kurichianil, J. "The Glory and the Cross. Jesus' Passion and Death in the Gospel of St. John," *ITS* 20 (1983) 5-15.

0454 Giblin, C. H. "Confrontations in John 18,1-27," *Bib* 65 (1984) 210-232.

0455 Robinson, J. A. T. "'His witness is true': A test of the Johannine claim," *Jesus and the Politics of His Day*. Ed. E. Bammel and C. F. D. Moule. Cambridge: 1984, 473-478.

0456 Ball, R. M. "S. John and the Institution of the Eucharist," *JSNT* 23 (1985) 59-68.

0457 Collins, R. F. "John's Gospel: A Passion Narrative," *BibToday* 24 (1986) 181-186.

0458 Fuller, R. H. "The Passion, Death and Resurrection of Jesus according to St. John," *Chicago Studies* 25 (1986) 51-63.

0459 Granskou, D. "Anti-Judaism in the Passion Accounts of the Fourth Gospel," *Anti-Judaism in Early Christianity: Volume 1. Paul and the Gospels*. Ed. P. Richardson and D. Granskou. Waterloo, Ont.: 1986, 210-216.

0460 Manns, F. "Le symbolisme du jardin dans le récit de la passion selon St Jean," *Studii Biblici Franciscani Liber Annuus* 37 (1987) 53-80.

0461 Culpepper, R. A. "The Death of Jesus: An Exegesis of John 19:28-37," *Faith and Mission* 5 (1988) 64-70.

0462 Garland, D. E. "John 18-19: Life Through Jesus' Death," *RevExp* 85 (1988) 485-499.

0463 Sullivan, R. "Jesus' Suffering, Death and Resurrection in the Fourth Gospel," *Theological Educator* 38 (1988) 104-120.

0464 Mahony, J. W. "The Crucifixion of and Resurrection of Jesus (John 18-21)," *Mid-America Journal* 12 (1988) 97-131.

See also 0226, 0228, 0229, 0230, 0285, 0373, 1131, 1141, 1150,
1159, 1167, 1175, 1179, 1241, 1298, 1315, 1336, 1367, 1396,
1534, 1544, 1547, 1549, 1551, 1554, 1556, 1560, 1565, 1570,
1577, 1578, 1588, 1593, 1599, 1601, 1607, 1609, 1610, 1611,
1612, 1616, 1620, 1624, 1629, 1630, 1642, 1643, 1644, 1645,
1646, 1647, 1649, 1652, 1653, 1654, 1656, 1661, 1746, 1755,
1762, 1767, 1795, 1796, 1798, 1802, 1803, 1805, 1811, 1814,
1816, 1823, 1824, 1825, 1827, 1906, 1934, 1979, 1981-2002,
2049, 2056

VII. The Chronology of the Passion

Books

0465 Chwolson, D. *Das letzte Passamahl Christi und der Tag seines Todes.* 2d. ed. Leipzig: 1908.

0466 Holzmeister, U. *Chronologia Vitae Christi.* Rome: 1933.

0467 Ogg, G. *The Chronology of the Public Ministry of Jesus.* Cambridge: 1940.

0468 Jaubert, A. *La Date de la Cène Calendrier Biblique et liturgie chrétienne.* Paris: 1957. Eng. trans.: *The Date of the Last Supper.* Trans. I. Rafferty. New York/London: 1965.

0469 Ruckstuhl, E. *Die Chronologie des letzten Mahles und des Leidens Jesu.* BibB 4. Einsiedeln: 1963. Eng. Trans.: *Chronology of the Last Days of Jesus.* Trans. V. J. Drapela. New York: 1965.

0470 Belcher, J. *In the Midst of the Week.* Indianapolis, IN.: 1967.

0471 Hoehner, H. W. *Chronological Aspects of the Life of Christ.* Grand Rapids: 1977.

0472 Goldstine, H. *New and Full Moons 1001 B.C. to A.D. 1651.* Philadelphia: 1973.

Articles

0473 Aberle. "Über den Tag des letzten Abendmahls," *TQ* 45 (1863) 537-568.

0474 Aldrich, J. K. "The Crucifixion on Thursday—Not Friday," *BSac* 27 (1870) 401-429.

0475 Caspari, C. E. "The Date of the Passion of Our Lord," *BSac* 27 (1870) 469-484.

0476 Wright, A. "On the Date of the Crucifixion," *Biblical World* 2 (1893) 7-14, 106-112, 167-177, 275-282.

0477 Gray, E. P. "The Last Passover and Its Harmonies," *BSac* 51 (1894) 339-346.

0478 Jones, R. G. "The Time of the Death and Resurrection of Jesus Christ," *BSac* 51 (1894) 505-511.

0479 Heisler, C. W. "On the Day of the Crucifixion of our Lord," *LQ* 25 (1895) 465-466.

0480 Belser, J. E. "Der Tag des letzten Abendmahls und des Todes Jesu," *TQ* 78 (1896) 529-576.

0481 Semeria, G. B. "Le jour de la mort de Jésus selon les synoptiques et selon saint Jean," *RB* 5 (1896) 78-87.

0482 Boys Smith, E. P. "The Date of the Crucifixion," *ExpT* 10 ((1898-99) 383-384.

0483 Masterman, E. W. G. "Was Our Lord Crucified on the 14th or 15th Nisan?" *ExpT* 10 (1898-99) 383-384.

0484 Box, G. H. "The Jewish Antecedents of the Eucharist," *JTS* 3 (1902) 357-369.

0485 Preuschen, E. "Todesjahr und Todestag Jesu," *ZNW* 5 (1904) 1-17.

0486 Grey, H. G. "A Suggestion on St. John xix.14," *Exp* 7th ser 2 (1906) 451-454.

0487 Bacon, B. W. "Lucan versus Johannine Chronology," *Exp* 7th ser. 3 (1907) 206-220.

0488 Smith, D. "The Day of the Crucifixion," *ExpT* 20 (1908-09) 514-518.

0489 Fotheringham, J. K. "Astronomical Evidence for the Date of the Crucifixion," *JTS* 12 (1910-11) 120-127.

0490 Gibson, M. "Which was the Night of the Passover?" *ExpT* 22 (1910-11) 378.

0491 Bromboszcz, T. "Der Einzug Jesu in Jerusalem bei Mondschein? Ein Beitrag zur chronologie der Leidensgeschichte," *BZ* 9 (1911) 164-170.

0492 Husband, R. W. "The Year of the Crucifixion," *Transactions of the American Philological Association* 46 (1915) 5-27.

0493 Linder, J. "Zur Frage nach dem Monatstage des letzten Abendmahles und Todes Christi," *ZKT* 39 (1915) 600-602.

0494 Suffrin, A. E. "The Last Supper and the Passover," *ExpT* 29 (1917-18) 475-477.

0495 Kissane, E. J. "Date of the Last Supper," *ITQ* 15 (1920) 365-368.

0496 Gerhardt, O. "Berichtigung," *Bib* 9 (1928) 464-465.

0497 Schaumberger, J. "Der 14. Nisan als Kreuzigungstag und die Synoptiker," *Bib* 9 (1928) 57-77.

0498 Schoch, K. "Christi Kreuzigung am 14. Nisan" *Bib* 9 (1928) 48-56.

0499 Schoch, K. "Entgegnung auf obige 'Berichtigung'," *Bib* 9 (1928) 466468.

0500 Gerhardt, O. "Das Datum der Kreuzigung Christi," *Astronomische Nachrichten* 240 (1930) 137-162; 242 (1931) 305-310.

0501 Torrey, C. C. "The Date of the Crucifixion according to the Fourth Gospel," *JBL* 50 (1931) 233-237.

0502 Christie, W. M. "Did Christ Eat the Passover with His Disciples? or, The Synoptics *versus* John's Gospel," *ExpT* 43 (1932) 515-519.

0503 Holzmeister, U. "Neuere Arbeiten über das Datum der Kreuzigung Christi," *Bib* 13 (1932) 93-103.

0504 Zeitlin, S. "The Date of the Crucifixion according to the Fourth Gospel," *JBL* 51 (1932) 263-268.

0505 Levie, J. "La Date de la Mort du Christ," *NRT* 60 (1933) 141-147.

0506 Dibelius, M. and Kohler, W. "Der Todestag Jesu," *Theologische Blätter* 13 (1934) 65-71.

0507 Fotheringham, J. K. "The Evidence of Astronomy and Technical Chronology for the Date of the Crucifixion," *JTS* 35 (1934) 146-162.

0508 Fotheringham, D. R. "Bible Chronology," *ExpT* 48 (1936-37) 234-235.

0509 McCubbin, J. H. "The Date of the Last Supper in the Synoptists and the Fourth Gospel," *Theology* 37 (1938) 178-180.

0510 Gilmer, G. "A Week in the Life of Christ," *BSac* 96 (1939) 42-50.

0511 Richardson, C. C. "Early Patristic Evidences for the Synoptic Chronology of the Passion," *ATR* 22 (1940) 299-308.

0512 Richardson, C. C. "The Quartodecimans and the Synoptic Chronology," *HTR* 33 (1940) 177-190.

0513 Doyle, A. D. "Pilate's Career and the Date of the Crucifixion," *JTS* 42 (1941) 190-193.

0514 Styler, G. M. "The Chronology of the Passion Narratives," *ATR* 23 (1941) 67-78.

0515 Hanson, R. P. C. "Further Evidence for Indications of the Johannine Chronology of the Passion to be Found in the Synoptic Evangelists," *ExpT* 53 (1941-42) 178-180.

0516 Amadon, G. "Ancient Jewish Calendation," *JBL* 61 (1942) 227-279.

0517 Kraeling, C. H. "Olmstead's Chronology of the Life of Christ," *ATR* 24 (1942) 334-354.

0518 Ogg, G. "Is A.D. 41 the Date of the Crucifixion?" *JTS* 43 (1942) 187-188.

0519 Feigin, S. I. "The Date of the Last Supper," *ATR* 25 (1943) 212-217.

0520 Heawood, P. J. "The Passover," *ExpT* 54 (1943) 330-331.

0521 Amadon, G. "The Crucifixion Calendar," *JBL* 63 (1944) 177-190.

0522 Parker, R. A. "Ancient Jewish Calendation, a Criticism," *JBL* 63 (1944) 173-176.

0523 Cerny, E. A. "Recent Studies on the Date of the Crucifixion," *CBQ* 7 (1945) 223-230.

0524 Heawood, P. J. "The Beginning of the Jewish Day," *JQR* 36 (1945) 393-401.

0525 Zeitlin, S. "The Beginning of the Jewish Day during the Second Commonwealth," *JQR* 36 (1945) 403-414.

0526 O'Herlihy, D. J. "The Year of the Crucifixion," *CBQ* 8 (1946) 298-305.

0527 Georgi, W. "Timelog of Jesus' Last Days," *CTM* 18 (1947) 263-277.

0528 Nolle, L. "Did Our Lord Eat the Pasch of the Old Testament before His Passion?" *Scr* 3 (1948) 43-45.

0529 Morgenstern, J. "The Reckoning of the Day in the Gospels and Acts," *Crozer Quarterly* 26 (1949) 232-240.

0530 Bratcher, R. G. "The Reckoning of Time in the Fourth Gospel," *RevExp* 48 (1951) 161-168.

0531 Heawood, P. J. "The Time of the Last Supper," *JQR* 42 (1951) 37-44.

0532 Robinson, E. W. B. "The Date and Significance of the Last Supper," *EvQ* 23 (1951) 126-133.

0533 Zeitlin, S. "The Time of the Passover Meal," *JQR* 42 (1951-52) 45-50.

0534 Zeitlin, S. "The Last Supper as an Ordinary Meal in the Fourth Gospel," *JQR* 42 (1951-52) 251-260.

0535 Bonsirven, J. "Hora Talmudica—la notation chronologique de Jean 19,14 aurait-elle und sens symbolique?" *Bib* 33 (1952) 511-515.

0536 Torrey, C. C. "In the Fourth Gospel the Last Supper was the Paschal Meal," *JQR* 42 (1952) 239-240.

0537 Jaubert, A. "Le Calendrier des Jubiles et de la Secte de Qumran," *VT* 3 (1953) 250-264.

0538 Jaubert, A. "La date de la dernière Cène," *RHR* 146 (1954) 140-173.

0539 Saarnivaara, U. "The Date of the Crucifixion in the Synoptics and John," *LQ* 6 (1954) 157-160.

0540 Jaubert, A. "The Calendar of Jubilees and of the Sect of Qumran," *TD* 5 (1957) 67-72.

0541 Johnston, L. "The Date of the Last Supper," *Scr* 9 (1957) 108-115.

0542 Barrett, C. K. "Luke XXII.15: To Eat the Passover," *JTS* 9 (1958) 305-307.

0543 Blinzler, J. "Qumran-Kalender und Passionschronologie," *ZNW* 49 (1958) 238-251.

0544 Gaechter, P. "Eine neue Chronologie der Leidenswoche?" *ZKT* 80 (1958) 555-561.

0545 MacRae, G. W. "A New Date for the Last Supper," *AER* 138 (1958) 294-302.

0546 O'Flynn, J. A. "The Date of the Last Supper," *ITQ* 25 (1958) 58-63.

0547 Skehan, P. W. "The Date of the Last Supper," *CBQ* 20 (1958) 192-199.

0548 Strobel, A. "Erwägungen zur Passions-Chronologie des Evangeliums," *ZNW* 49 (1958) 195-196.

0549 Walther, J. A. "The Chronology of Passion Week," *JBL* 77 (1958) 116-122.

0550 Black, M. "The Arrest and Trial of Jesus and the Date of the Last Supper," *New Testament Essays*. Ed. A. J. B. Higgins (Fest. T. W. Manson). Manchester: 1959, 18-33.

0551 Mann, C. S. "The Chronology of the Passion and the Qumran Calendar," *ChQR* 160 (1959) 149-159.

0552 McDonald, R. F. "The Last Supper: Thursday or Tuesday," *AER* 140 (1959) 79-92; 168-181.

0553 Ogg, G. "Review of Mlle. Jaubert, *La date de la Cène*," *NovT* 3 (1959) 149-160.

0554 Walker, N. "Concerning the Jaubertian Chronology of the Passion," *NovT* 3 (1959-60) 317-320.

0555 Jaubert, A. "Jésus et la calendrier de Qumran," *NTS* 7 (1960-61) 1-30.

0556 Montefiore, H. "When Did Jesus Die?" *ExpT* 72 (1960) 53-54.

0557 Strobel, A. "Der Termin des Todes Jesu. Überschau und Lösungsvorschlag unter Einschluss des Qumrankalenders," *ZNW* 51 (1960) 69-101.

0558 Walker, N. "The Reckoning of Hours in the Fourth Gospel," *NovT* 4 (1960) 69-73.

0559 Walker, N. "Jaubert's Solution of the Holy Week Problem," *ExpT* 72 (1960-61) 93-94.

0560 Kuhn, K. G. "Zum essenischen Kalendar," *ZNW* 52 (1961) 65-73.

0561 Shepherd, M. H. "Are Both the Synoptics and John Correct about the Date of Jesus' Death?" *JBL* 80 (1961) 123-132.

0562 Cadman, W. H. "The Christian Pascha and the Day of the Crucifixion—Nisan 14 or 15?" *Studia Patristica* V (TU 80 1962) 8-16.

0563 Freedman, D. N. "When Did Christ Die? New Light from the DSS on the Date of the Last Supper and the Events of the Holy Week," *Pittsburgh Perspective* 3 (1962) 52-57.

0564 Mahoney, J. "The Last Supper and the Qumran Calendar," 48 (1963) 216-232.

0565 Walker, N. "Pauses in the Passion Story and their Significance for Chronology, *NovT* 6 (1963) 16-19.

0566 Walker, N. "Yet Another Look at the Passion Chronology," *NovT* 6 (1963) 286-289.

0567 Zeitlin, S. "I. The Dates of the Birth and the Crucifixion of Jesus," *JQR* 55 (1964) 1-22.

0568 Carmignac, J. "Comment Jésus et ses contemporains pouvaient-ils célébrer la Pâque á une date non officielle?" *RevQ* 5 (1964-65) 59-79.

0569 Ogg, G. "The Chronology of the Last Supper," *Historicity and Chronology in the New Testament*. London: 1965 75-96.

0570 Stroes, H. R. "Does the Day Begin in the Evening or Morning?" *VT* 16 (1966) 460-475.

0571 Jaubert, A. "Le mercredi où Jésus fut livré," *NTS* 14 (1967-68) 145-164.

0572 Maier, P. L. "Sejanus, Pilate, and the Date of the Crucifixion," *Church History* 37 (1968) 3-13.

0573 Beckwith, R. T. "The Day, its Divisions and its Limits, in Biblical Thought," *EvQ* 43 (1971) 218-227.

0574 Jaubert, A. "The Calendar of Qumran and the Passion Narrative in John," *John and Qumran*. Ed. J. H. Charlesworth. London: 1972, 62-75.

0575 Hoehner, H. W. "Chronological Aspects of the Life of Christ, Part IV: The Day of Christ's Crucifixion," *BSac* 131 (1974) 241-264.

0576 Hoehner, H. W. "Chronological Aspects of the Life of Christ, Part V: The Day of Christ's Crucifixion," *BSac* 131 (1974) 332-348.

0577 Rusk, R. "The Day He Died," *ChrTod* 18 (1974) 720-722.

0578 Chenderlin, F. "Distributed Observance of the Passover—A Preliminary Test of the Hypothesis," *Bib* 57 (1976) 1-24.

0579 Dockx, S. "Le 14 Nisan de l'an 30," *Chronologies néotestamentaires et vie de l'Église primitive. Recherches exégétiques*. Gembloux: 1976, 21-29.

0580 Dockx, S. "Chronologie du dernier jour de la vie de Jésus," *Chronologies neotestamentaires et vie de l'Église primitive. Recherches exegetiques*. Gembloux: 1976, 31-43.

0581 Dubois, J. D. "Chronique johannique," *ETR* 51 (1976) 373-381.

0582 Mulder, H. "John xviii 28 and the Date of the Crucifixion," *Miscellanea Neotestamentica*. Ed. T. Baarda, A. F. J. Klijn, amd W. C. Van Unnik. *NovTSup* 48. Leiden: 1978, 87-106.

0583 Vanderkam, J. C. "The Origin, Character, and Early History of the 364-Day Calendar: A Reassessment of Jaubert's Hypothesis," *CBQ* 41 (1979) 390-411.

0584 Humphreys, C. J. and Waddington, W. G. "Dating the Crucifixion," *Nature* 306 (1983) 743-746.

0585 Ruckstuhl, E. "Zur Chronologie der Leidensgeschichte Jesu," *SNTU* 10 (1985) 27-61.

0586 Hoehner, H. W. "Jesus' Last Supper," *Essays in Honor of J. Dwight Pentecost*. Ed. S. D. Toussaint and C. H. Dyer. Chicago: 1986, 63-74.

0587 Ruckstuhl, E. "Zur Chronologie der Leidensgeschichte Jesu (II. Teil)," *SNTU* 11 (1986) 97-129.

VIII. The Anointing at Bethany (Matt 26:6-13; Mark 14:3-9)

Articles

0588 Elmslie, W. G. "At the Sign of the Bible," *Exp* 3d ser., 7 (1898) 395-397.

0589 Nestle, E. "Die unverfälschte köstliche Narde," *ZNW* 3 (1902) 169-171.

0590 Goetz, K. G. "Zur Salbung Jesu in Bethanien," *ZNW* 4 (1903) 88.

0591 Linder, G. "Zur Salbung Jesu in Bethanien," *ZNW* 4 (1903) 179-181.

0592 Preuschen, E. "Die Salbung Jesu in Bethanien," *ZNW* 4 (1903) 88.

0593 Van Veldhuizen, A. "Die alabastern Flasche," *TStudien* 25 (1907) 170-172.

0594 Lagrange, M. J. "Jésus a-t-il été oint plusieurs fois et par plusieurs femmes? Opinions des anciens écrivains ecclésiastiques (Luc, vii,36-50, Matthieu, xxvi,6-13; Marc, xiv,3-9; Jean, xii,1-8; cf. Jean, xi,2)," *RB* 9 (1912) 504-532.

0595 van der Flier, A. "Markus 14,2," *TStudien* 29 (1911) 109-111.

0596 Grubb, E. "The Anointing of Jesus," *ExpT* 26 (1914) 461-463.

0597 von Sybel, L. "Die Salbungen, Mt. 26,6-13, Mc. 14,3-9, Lc. 7,36-50, Joh. 12,1-8," *ZNW* 23 (1924) 184-193.

0598 Bevan, T. W. "The Four Anointings," *ExpT* (1927-28) 137-139.

0599 Wood, J. A. "The Anointing at Bethany and its Significance," *ExpT* 39 (1927-28) 475-476.

0600 Jeremias, J. "Die Salbungsgeschichte (Mc. 14:3-9)," *ZNW* 35 (1936) 75-82. = *Abba. Studien zur neutestamentlichen Theologie und Zeitgeschichte*. Göttingen: 107-115.

0601 Kilpatrick, G. D. "*Epanō* Mark 14:5," *JTS* 42 (1941) 181-182.

0602 Kilpatrick, G. D. "*Epanō* Mark xiv.5, an Addendum," *JTS* 45 (1944) 177.

0603 Köbert, R. "Nardos Pistike-Kostnarde," *Bib* 29 (1948) 279-281.

0604 Lee, G. M. "St. Mark XIV.7," *ExpT* 61 (1949-50) 160.

0605 Daube, D. "The Anointing at Bethany and Jesus Burial," *ATR* 32 (1950) 186-199 = *The New Testament and Rabbinic Judaism*. London: 1956, 310-324.

0606 Schnackenburg, R. "Der johanneische Bericht von der Salbung in Bethanien Joh. 12,1-8" *MTZ* 1 (1950) 48-52.

0607 Jeremias, J. "Mc 14:9," *ZNW* 44 (1952-53) 103-107.

0608 Legault, A. "An Application of the Form-Critique Method to the Anointings," *CBQ* 16 (1954) 131-145.

0609 Bauer, J. B. "Ut Quid Perditio Ista? Zu Mk. 14,4f u. Parr." *NovT* 3 (1959) 54-56.

0610 Sahlin, H. "Zwei Fälle von harmonisierenden Einfluss das Matthäus—Evangeliums auf das Markus—Evangelium," *ST* 13 (1959) 166-179.

0611 Greenlee, J. H. "*Eis mnēmosynen autēs*, 'For her Memorial' Mt. 26:13; Mk. 14:9," *ExpT* 71 (1959-60) 245.

0612 Nesbitt, C. F. "The Bethany Traditions in the Gospel Narratives," *JBR* 29 (1961) 119-124.

0613 Derrett, J. D. M. "The Anointing at Bethany," *SE* II (TU 87 1964) 174-182. = *Law in the New Testament*. London: 1970, 266-275.

0614 Danker, F. W. "The Literary Unity of Mark 14:1-25," *JBL* 85 (1966) 467-472.

0615 Delobel, J. "L'onction par la pécheresse," *ETL* 42 (1966) 415-475.

0616 Storch, R. " 'Was soll diese Verschwendung?' Bemerkungen zur Auslegungsgeschichte von Mk. 14:4f," *Der Ruf Jesu und die Antwort der Gemeinde*. Ed. E. Lohse (Fest. J. Jeremias). Göttingen: 1970, 247-258.

0617 Pesch, R. "Die Salbung Jesu in Bethanien (Mk. 14,3-9). Eine Studie zur Passionsgeschichte," *Orientierung an Jesus*. Ed. P. Hoffmann, N. Brox, and W. Pesch (Fest. J. Schmid). Freiburg: 1973, 267-285.

0618 Wilckens, U. "Vergebung für die Sünderin (Luk. 7:36-50)," *Orientierung an Jesus*. Ed. P. Hoffmann, N. Brox, and W. Pesch. (Fest. J. Schmid). Freiburg: 1973, 394-424.

0619 Elliott, J. K. "The Anointing of Jesus," *ExpT* 85 (1974) 105-107.

0620 Feuillet, A. "Les deux onctions faites sur Jésus, et Marie-Madeleine," *RevThom* 75 (1975) 357-394.

0621 Holst, R. "The One Anointing of Jesus: Another Application of the Form-Critical Method," *JBL* 95 (1976) 435-446.

0622 Platt, E. E. "The Ministry of Mary of Bethany," *TToday* 34 (1977) 29-39.

0623 Munro, W. "The Anointing in Mark 14:3-9 and John 12:1-8," SBLASP (1979) 1:127-130.

0624 Schedl, C. "Die Salbung Jesu in Betanien. Zur kompositionskunst von Mk. 14,3-9 und Mt. 26,6-13," *BLit* 54 (1981) 151-162.

0625 März, C. P. "Zur Traditionsgeschichte von Mk. 14,3-9 und Parallel," *SNTU* 6-7 (1982) 89-122.

0626 Schnider, F. "Christusverkündigung und Jesuserzählungen. Exegetische Überlegungen zu Mk 14,3-9," *Kairos* 24 (1982) 171-180.

0627 Delorme, J. "Sémiotique du récit et récit de la Passion," *RSR* 73 (1985) 85-109.

0628 Motyer, C. J. "A Sitz im Leben for Mark 14:9," *ExpT* 99 (1987) 78-80.

0629 Thiemann, R. F. "The Unnamed Woman at Bethany," *TToday* 44 (1987-88) 179-188.

0630 Beavis, M. A. "Women as Models of Faith in Mark," *BTB* 18 (1988) 3-9.

0631 Grassi, J. A. "The Secret Heroine of Mark's Drama," *BTB* 18 (1988) 10-15.

See also 0271, 0308

IX. The Last Supper and the Passover

Books

0632 Oesterley, W. O. E. *The Jewish Background of the Christian Liturgy*. Oxford: 1925.

0633 Gavin, F. *The Jewish Antecedents of the Christian Sacraments*. London: 1928.

0634 Jeremias, J. *Die Passahfeier der Samaritaner*. BZAW 59. Giessen: 1932.

0635 Lohse, B. *Das Passafest der Quartadecimaner*. BFCT 43. Gütersloh: 1953.

0636 Segal, J. B. *The Hebrew Passover*. London: 1963.

0637 Feneberg, R. *Christliche Passafeier und Abendmahl*. SANT 27. Munich: 1971.

0637a Saldarini, A. J. *Jesus and Passover*. New York: 1984.

Articles

0638 Hailer, M. "Das Heilige Abendmahl und das Passahmahl," *Theologische Studien aus Württemberg* 8 (1887) 68-

0639 Schmidt, N. "The Character of Christ's Last Meal," *JBL* 11 (1892) 1-21.

0640 Selby, T. G. "The Passover and the Lord's Supper," *Exp* 9 (1899) 210-217.

0641 Box, G. H. "The Jewish Antecedents of the Eucharist," *JTS* 3 (1901-02) 357-369.

0642 Volz, P. "Ein heutiger Passahabend," *ZNW* 7 (1906) 247-251.

0643 Milligan, G. "The Last Supper not a Paschal Meal," *ExpT* 20 (1908-09) 334.

0644 Allen, W. C. "The Last Supper was a Passover Meal," *ExpT* 20 (1908-09) 377.   ·

0645 Frederick, W. "Did Jesus Eat the Passover?" *BibSac* 68 (1911) 503-509.

0646 Burkitt, F. C. "The Last Supper and the Paschal Meal," *JTS* 17 (1915-16) 291-297.

0647 Suffrin, A. E. "The Last Supper and the Passover," *ExpT* 29 (1917-18) 475-477.

0648 Lietzmann, H. "Jüdische Passahsitten und der *aphikomenos*. Kritische Randnoten zu R. Eislers Aufsatz über 'Das letzte Abendmahl'," *ZNW* 25 (1926) 1-5.

0649 Marmorstein, A. "Das letzte Abendmahl und der Sederabend," *ZNW* 25 (1926) 1-5.

0650 Dalman, G. "The Passover Meal," *Jesus-Jeshua*. Trans. P. R. Levertoff. London: 1929, 86-184.

0651 Coppens, J. "Les soi-disant analogies juives de l'Eucharistie," *ETL* 8 (1931) 238-248.

0652 Jeremias, J. "Das Brotbrechen beim Passahmahl und Mc. 14.22 par.," *ZNW* 33 (1934) 203-204.

0653 Heawood, P. J. "The Last Passover in the Gospels," *ExpT* 53 (1941-42) 295-297.

0654 Thiele, E. R. "The Day and Hour of Passover Observance in New Testament Times," *ATR* 28 (1946) 163-168.

0655 Preiss, T. "Le dernier repas de Jésus fut-il un repas pascal?" *TZ* 4 (1948) 81-101.

0656 Daube, D. "Two Notes on the Passover 'Haggadah'," *JTS* 50 (1949) 53-57.

0657 Rosenthal, J. "Passover and the Festival of Unleavened Bread," *JJS* 3 (1952) 178-179.

0658 Zeitlin, S. "The Last Supper as an Ordinary Meal in the Fourth Gospel," *JQR* 42 (1952) 251-260.

0659 Delorme, J. "La céne et la pâque dans le Nouveau Testament," *Lumière et Vie* 31 (1957) 9-48.

0660 Barrett, C. K. "Luke xxii.15: To Eat the Passover," *JTS* 9 (1958) 305-307.

0661 Hruby, K. "La pâque juive du temps du Christi à la lumière des documents de la littérature rabbinique," *OrSyr* 6 (1961) 81-94.

0662 Dockx, S. "Le récit du repas pascal Marc 14,17-26," *Bib* 46 (1965) 445-453.

0663 Barosse, T. "The Passover and the Paschal Meal," *The Breaking of Bread*. Ed. P. Benoit et.al. Concilium 40. New York: 1969, 23-24.

0664 Bahr, G. J. "The Seder of Passover and the Eucharistic Words," *NovT* 12 (1970) 181-202.

0665 Lapide, P. E. "Der mysterlose Mazzabrocken. Ging der Eucharistiefeier ein Pessachritus voraus?" *LMH* 14 (1975) 120-124.

0666 Davies, P. R. "Passover and the Dating of the Aqedah," *JJS* 30 (1979) 59-67.

0667 Senn, F. C. "The Lord's Supper, Not the Passover Seder," *Worship* 60 (1986) 362-368.

0668 Bokser, B. M. "Was the Last Supper a Passover Seder?" *Bible Review* 3 (1987) 24-33.

See also 0382, 0416, 0429, 0465, 0473, 0477, 0480, 0484, 0490, 0495, 0502, 0509, 0519, 0520, 0528, 0531, 0532, 0533, 0534, 0536, 0538, 0541, 0545, 0546, 0552, 0562, 0563, 0564 0568, 0569, 0578, 0586, 0690, 0692, 0702, 0721, 0754, 0756, 0766, 0856, 0864, 0955

X. The Last Supper, On the Way to Gethsemane

Books

0669 Haupt, E. *Über die ursprüngliche Form und Bedeutung der Abend-mahlsworte.* Halle: 1894.

0670 Schultzen, F. *Das Abendmahl im Neuen Testament.* Göttingen: 1895.

0671 Hoffmann, R. A. *Die Abendmahls Gedanken Jesu Christi.* Königs-berg: 1896.

0672 Eichorn, A. *Das Abendmahl im Neuen Testament.* Christliche Welt 36 supp. Leipzig: 1898.

0673 Clemen, C. *Der Ursprung des heiligen Abendmahls.* Leipzig: 1898.

0674 Hehn, J. *Die Einsetzung des heiligen Abendmahls als Beweis für die Gottheit Christi.* Würzburg: 1900.

0675 Berning, W. *Die Einsetzung der hl. Eucharistie in ihrer ursprün-glichen Form nach den Berichten des Neuen Testaments kritisch untersucht.* Münster: 1901.

0676 Schweitzer, A. *Das Abendmahlsproblem auf Grund der wissen-schaftlichen Forschung des 19. Jahrhunderts und der histo-rischen Berichte.* Tübingen: 1901. = *The Problem of the Lord's Supper.* Trans. A. J. Mattill, Jr. Macon: 1982.

0677 Goetz, K. G. *Die heutige Abendmahlsfrage in ihrer geschichtlichen Entwicklung.* 2d ed. Leipzig: 1907.

0678 Reville, J. *Les origins de l'eucharistie, messe, saint céne.* Paris: 1908.

0679 Goguel, M. *L'euchariste des origines à Justin Martyr.* Paris: 1910.

0680 Goetz, K. G. *Das Abendmahl, eine Diathēkē Jesu oder sein letztes Gleichnis?* UNT 8. Leipzig: 1920.

0681 Frischkopf, B. *Erörterungen über die Abendmahlsfrage*. Münster: 1921.

0682 MacGregor, G. H. C. *Eucharistic Origins*. London: 1928.

0683 Goetz, K. G. *Der Ursprung des kirchlichen Abendmahls blosse Mahlgemeinschaft von Jesus und seiner Jüngern oder eine besondere Handlung und Worte von Jesus?* Basel: 1929.

0684 Goossens, W. *Les origines de l'Eucharistie, sacrement et sacrifice*. Gembloux/Paris: 1931.

0685 Maxfield, T. H. W. *The Words of Institution*. Cambridge: 1933.

0686 Cullmann, O. *La signification de la sainte-céne dans le christianisme primitif*. Strasbourgh: 1936.

0687 Arnold, A. *Der Ursprung des christlichen Abendmahls im Lichte der neuesten liturgiegeschichtlichen Forschung*. Freiburg; 1937.

0688 Cirlot, F. L. *The Early Eucharist*. London: 1939.

0689 Gaugler, E. *Das Abendmahl im Neuen Testament*. Basel: 1943.

0690 Barth, M. *Das Abendmahl. Passamahl Bundesmahl und Messiasmahl*. Zurich: 1945.

0691 Leenhardt, F. J. *Le Sacrament de la Sainte Céne*. Neuchatel: 1948.

0692 Walther, G. *Jesus das Passalamm des neuen Bundes. Der Zentralgedanke des Herrenmahles*. Gütersloh: 1950.

0693 Higgins, A. J. B. *The Lord's Supper in the New Testament*. London: 1952.

0694 Lessing, H. *Die Abendmahlsprobleme im Lichte der neutestamentlichen Forschung seit 1900*. Bonn: 1953.

0695 Schürmann, H. *Der Paschamahlbericht Lk. 22,(7-14) 15-18*. NTAbh 19. Münster: 1953.

0696 Schürmann, H. *Der Einsetzungsbericht Lk. 22:19-20*. NTAbh 20. Münster: 1955.

0697 Schürmann, H. *Jesu Abschiedsrede Lk. 22,21-38*. NTAbh 20. Münster: 1957.

0698 Neuenzeit, P. *Das Herrenmahl*. Munich: 1960.

0699 Marxsen, W. *Das Abendmahl als christologisches Problem*. Gütersloh: 1963. Eng. trans.: *The Lord's Supper as a Christological Problem*. Trans. L. Nieting. Philadelphia: 1970.

0700 Hook, N. *The Eucharist in the New Testament*. London: 1964.

0701 Du Toit, A. B. *Der Aspekt der Freude im urchristlichen Abendmahl*. Winterthur: 1965.

0702 Jeremias, J. *Die Abendmahlsworte Jesu.* 4th ed. Göttingen: 1967. Eng. trans.: *The Eucharistic Words of Jesus.* Trans. N. Perrin. London: 1963.

0703 Barclay, W. *The Lord's Supper.* 2nd ed. Philadelphia: 1969.

0704 Schürmann, H. *Jesu Abendsmahlshandlung als Zeichen für die Welt. Drei Vorträge.* Leipzig: 1970.

0705 Patsch, H. *Abendmahl und historischer Jesus.* Stuttgart: 1972.

0706 Wanke, J. *Beobachtungen zum Eucharistieverständnis des Lukas auf Grund der lukanischer Mahlberichte.* ETS 8. Leipzig: 1973.

0707 Schenker, A. *Das Abendmahl Jesu als Brennpunkt des Alten Testaments. Begegnung zwischen den beiden Testamenten. Eine bibeltheologische Skizze.* BibB 13. Fribourg: 1977.

0708 Pesch, R. *Wie Jesus die Abendmahl heilt. Der Grund der Eucharistie.* 2d ed. Freiburg/Basel/Vienna: Herder, 1978.

0709 Pesch, R. *Das Abendmahl und Jesus Todesverständnis.* 80. Freiburg/Basel/Vienna: Herder, 1978.

0710 Badia, L. F. *The Dead Sea People's Sacred Meal and Jesus' Last Supper.* Washington: 1979.

0711 Lietzmann, H. *Mass and Lord's Supper: A Study in the History of the Liturgy.* Trans. and rev. R. D. Richardson. Leiden: 1979.

0712 Kahlefeld, H. *Das Abschiedsmahl Jesu und die Eucharistie der Kirche.* Frankfurt: 1980.

0713 Marshall, I. H. *Last Supper and Lord's Supper.* Grand Rapids: 1980.

0714 Feeley-Harnik, G. *The Lord's Supper.* Philadelphia: 1981.

0715 Léon-Dufour, X. *Le Partage du Pain Eucharistique.* Paris: 1982. Eng. trans.: *Sharing the Eucharistic Bread: The Witness of the New Testament.* Trans. M. J. O'Connell. New York: 1987.

0716 Kilpatrick, G. D. *The Eucharist in Bible and Liturgy.* Cambridge: 1983.

0717 Barth, M. *Das Mahl des Herrn. Gemeinschaft mit Israel, mit Christus und unter den Gasten.* Neukirchen/Vluyn: 1987.

Articles

0718 Plummer, A. "This Do in Remembrance of Me" *Exp* 3d ser. 7 (1888) 441-449.

0719 Plummer, A. "St. Mark xiv.14, 15; St. Luke xxii.11, 12," *ExpT* 2 (1890-91) 81-82.

0720 MacMillan, H. "The Man Bearing a Pitcher of Water," *ExpT* 3 (1891-92) 58-60.

0721 Blass, F. "Zu Luk. 22,15ff.," *TSK* 69 (1897) 733-737.

0722 Johnston, J. B. "Professor Blass and St. Luke on the Lord's Supper," *ExpT* 9 (1897-98) 520.

0723 Sayce, A. H. "The Four Ways of Understanding the Words of Institution," *ExpT* 11 (1899-1900) 564-565.

0724 Wrede, W. "*To haima mou tēs diathēkēs*," *ZNW* 1 (1900) 69-74.

0725 Gray, W. A. "The Three Cups," *ExpT* 12 (1900-01) 295-299.

0726 Coffin, C. P. "Two sources for the Synoptic Account of the Last Supper," *AJT* 5 (1901) 102-116.

0727 Holtzmann, O. "Zu Lukas 22,20," *ZNW* 3 (1902) 359.

0728 Nestle, E. "Zu Lukas 22,20," *ZNW* 3 (1902) 252-253.

0729 Rauch, E. "Bemerkungen zum Markustexte. Mc 14,12-17," *ZNW* 3 (1902) 308-314.

0730 Blakiston, H. E. D. "The Lukan Account of the Institution of the Lord's Supper," *JTS* 4 (1902-03) 548-555.

0731 Holtzmann, O. "Das Abendmahl im Urchristentum," *ZNW* 5 (1904) 89-120.

0732 Nestle, E. " 'This do in Remembrance of Me'." *ExpT* 16 (1904-05) 144.

0733 Koch, W. "Die neutestamentlichen Abendmahlsberichte und die neueste Abendmahlsforschung," *TQ* 87 (1905) 230-257.

0734 Andersen, A. "Zu Mt. 26,17ff und Lc. 22,15 ff.," *ZNW* 7 (1906) 87-90.

0735 Andersen, A. "Mt. 26,26 f. und Parallelstellen im Lichte der Abendmahlslehre Justins," *ZNW* 7 (1906) 172-175.

0736 Nestle, E. "Zu Lc. 22,20," *ZNW* 7 (1906) 256-257.

0737 Wellhausen, J. "*Arton eklasen*, Mc. 14,22," *ZNW* 7 (1906) 182.

0738 Wohlenberg, G. "Die biblischen Abendmahlsberichte und ihre neure Kritik," *Neue kirchliche Zeitschrift* 17 (1906) 181-199, 247-251, 358-367.

0739 Burkitt, F. C. and Brooke, A. E. "St. Luke XXII.15, 16: What is the General Meaning?" *JTS* 9 (1908) 569-572.

0740 Eager, A. R. "St. Luke's Account of the Last Supper: A Critical Note on the Second Sacrament," *Exp* 7th ser. 4 (1908) 252-262, 343-361.

0741 Box, G. H. "St. Luke xxii.15, 16," *JTS* 10 (1908-09) 106-107.

0742 Robinson, H. M. "The Text of Luke xxii.17-25," *PTR* 8 (1910) 613-656.

0743 Tuker, M. A. R. "The Words of Institution as the Last Supper," *HibJ* 9 (1910-11) 134-135.

0744 Bernhard, S. "War Judas der Verräter bei der Einsetzung der hl. Eucharistie gegenwärtig?" *ZKT* 35 (1911) 30-65.

0745 Meinertz, M. "Zur Frage nach der Anwesenheit des Verräters Judas bei der Einsetzung der Eucharistie," *BZ* 9 (1911) 372-390.

0746 Todd, J. C. " 'Do This in Remembrance of Me'," *ExpT* 23 (1911-12) 378-379.

0747 Bacon, B. W. "The Lukan Tradition of the Lord's Supper," *HTR* 5 (1912) 322-348.

0748 Bernhard, S. "Nochmals über die Frage von der Gegenwart des Verräters bei der Einsetzung der hl. Eucharistie," *ZKT* 36 (1912) 411-416.

0749 Grass, K. "Zu Mc. 14,28," *ZNW* 13 (1912) 175-176.

0750 Loeschke, G. "Zur Frage nach der Einsetzung und Herkunft der Eucharistie," *ZWT* 54 (1912) 193-205.

0751 Gibson, M. D. "The House in which the Last Supper Was Held," *JTS* 17 (1915-16) 398.

0752 Goetz, K. G. "Abendmahl und Messopfer," *Schweizerische Theologische Zeitschrift* 35 (1918) 15-24.

0753 Haupt, P. "The Last Supper," *JBL* 40 (1921) 178-180.

0754 Doller, J. "Der Wein in Bibel und Talmud," *Bib* 4 (1923) 143-167; 267-299.

0755 Lock, W. "Studies in Texts," *Theology* 7 (1923) 284-285.

0756 von Sybel, L. "Das letzte Mahl Jesu," *TSK* 95 (1923-24) 116-124.

0757 Eisler, G. "Das letzte Abendmahl," *ZNW* 24 (1925) 161-192.

0758 Kittel, G. "Die Wirkungen des Christlichen Abendmahls nach dem Neuen Testament," *TSK* 97 (1925) 215-237.

0759 Monks, G. G. "The Lucan Account of the Last Supper," *JBL* 44 (1925) 228-260.

0760 Delporte, L. "Un texte de Saint Luc sur notre solidarité avec le Christ (Ev. 22,15-37)," *ETL* 3 (1926) 475-492.

0761 Bate, H. N. "The 'Shorter Text' of St. Luke xxii.15-20," *JTS* 28 (1926-27) 362-368.

0762 Burkitt, F. C. "On Luke xxii.17-20," *JTS* 28 (1926-27) 178-181.

0763 Barton, G. A. "The Eucharist," *Studies in the New Testament*. Philadelphia: 1928, 102-115.

0764 Joüon, P. "Notes philologiques sur les Évangiles.—Luc 22,29 (et 19,12; 23,42)," *RSR* 8 (1928) 355.

0765 Lecler, J. "L'argument des deux glaives (Luc xxii,38) dans les controverses politiques du moyen age," *RSR* 11 (1931) 299-339; 12 (1932) 151-177, 380-403.

0766 Moehlmann, C. H. "The Origin of the Lord's Supper," *Religion in Life* 2 (1933) 571-582.

0767 Morris, A. E. "Jesus and the Eucharist," *Theology* 26 (1933) 242-266.

0768 Dieu, L. "Prima die azymorum (Math. XXVI,17; Marc. XIV,12)," *ETL* 14 (1937) 657-667.

0769 Lohmeyer, E. "Das Abendmahl in der Urgemeinde," *JBL* 56 (1937) 217-252.

0770 Lohmeyer, E. "Vom urchristlichen Abendmahl," *TRu* 9 (1937) 168-227, 273-312; 10 (1938) 81-99.

0771 Benoit, P. "Le récit de la céne dans Lc. xxii,15-20 (étude de critique textuelle et littéraire)," *RB* 48 (1939) 357-393.

0772 Goetz, K. "Das vorausweisende Demonstrativum in Lc. 22,19-20 und 1 Cor. 11,24," *ZNW* 38 (1939) 188-190.

0773 McDowell, E. A. "Exegetical Notes," *RevExp* 38 (1941) 44-48.

0774 Preisker, H. "Der Verrat des Judas und das Abendmahl," *ZNW* 41 (1942) 151-155.

0775 Wright, R. F. "Studies in Texts," *Theology* 44 (1942) 296-300.

0776 Black, M. "The 'Fulfillment' in the Kingdom of God," *ExpT* 57 (1945-46) 25-26.

0777 Kilpatrick, G. D. "Luke xxii.19b-20," *JTS* 47 (1946) 49-56.

0778 Schweizer, E. "Das Abendmahl eine Vergegenwärtigung des Todes Jesu oder ein eschatologisches Freudenmahl?" *TZ* 2 (1946) 81-101.

0779 Seierstad, I. P. "Lukas 22,14-20," *TTKi* 18 (1947) 83-107.

0780 Black, M. "The Cup Metaphor in Mk. 14,36," *ExpT* 59 (1947-48) 195.

0781 Jeremias, J. "Zur Exegese der Abendmahlsworte Jesu," *EvT* 7 (1947-48) 60-63.

0782 Benoit, P. "Luc xxii.19b-20," *JTS* 49 (1948) 145-147.

0783 Bonsirven, J. "Hoc est corpus meum. Recherches sur l'original araméen," *Bib* 29 (1948) 205-219.

0784 Cullmann, O. "Neutestamentliche Wortforschung. *HYPER (ANTI) POLLEN*," *TZ* 4 (1948) 93-104.

0785 Throckmorton, B. H., Jr. "The Longer Reading of Luke 22:19b-20," *ATR* 30 (1948) 55-56.

0786 Jeremias, J. "Zur Exegese der Abendmahlsworte Jesu," *Nuntius sodalicii neotestamentici Uppsaliensis* 1 (1949) 3-5.

0787 Jeremias, J. "The Last Supper," *JTS* 50 (1949) 1-10.

0788 Kuhn, K. G. "Die Abendmahlsworte," *TLZ* 75 (1950) 399-407.

0789 Vogels, H. "Mk. 14:25 und Parallelen," *Vom Wort des Lebens* NTAbh 1 (Fest. M. Meinertz). Münster: 1951, 93-104.

0790 Kuhn, K. G. "Über den ursprünglichen Sinn des Abendmahls und sein Verhältnis zu den Gemeinschaftsmahlen der Sektenschrift," *EvT* 10 (1950-51) 508-527. Eng. trans.: "The Lord's Supper and the Communal Meal at Qumran," *The Scrolls and the New Testament*. Ed. K. Stendahl. New York: 1958, 65-93; 259-65.

0791 Schürmann, H. "Die Semitismen im Einsetzungsbericht bei Markus und bei Lukas (Mk. 14,22-24/ Lk. 22,19-20)," *ZKT* 73 (1951) 72-77.

0792 Schürmann, H. "Lk. 22,19b-20—als ursprüngliche Textüberlieferung," *Bib* 32 (1951) 364-392, 522-541. = *Traditionsgeschichtliche Untersuchungen zu den Synoptischen Evangelien*. Düsseldorf: 1968, 1:159-197.

0793 Foster, J. "Go and make ready (Luke xxii.8, John xiv. 2)," *ExpT* 63 (1951-52) 193.

0794 Marxsen, W. "Repräsentation im Abendmahl?" *MPT* 41 (1952) 69-78.

0795 Schäfer, K. T. "Zur Textgeschichte von Lk. 22,19b, 20," *Bib* 33 (1952) 237-239.

0796 Schürmann, H. "Lk. 22,42a, das älteste Zeugnis für Lk. 22,20?" *MTZ* 3 (1952) 185-188.

0797 Delekat, F. "Methodenkritische und dogmatische Probleme angesichts der gegenwärtigen Exegese der neutestamentlichen Abendmahlstexte," *EvT* 12 (1952-53) 389-415.

0798 Jeremias, J. "The Last Supper," *ExpT* 64 (1952-53) 91-92.

0799 Kilpatrick, G. D. "The Last Supper," *ExpT* 64 (1952-53) 4-8.

0800 Marxsen, W. "Der Ursprung des Abendmahls," *EvT* 12 (1952-53) 293-303.

0801 Schweizer, E. "Das johanneische Zeugnis vom Herrenmahl," *EvT* 12 (1952-53) 341-363.

0802 Dewar, L. "The Biblical Use of the Term 'Blood'," *JTS* 4 (1953) 204-208.

0803 Mascall, E. L. "The Body and the Blood of Christ," *CQR* 154 (1953) 53-60.

0804 Morris, L. "The Biblical Use of the Term 'Blood,'" *JTS* 3 (1953) 216-227.

0805 Sutcliffe, E. F. " 'Et tu alquando conversus,' St. Luke 22,32," *CBQ* 15 (1953) 305-310.

0806 Kreck, W. "Die reformierte Abendmahlslehre angesichts der heutigen exegetischen Situation," *EvT* 14 (1954) 193-211.

0807 Schweizer, E. "Das Herrenmahl im Neuen Testament," *TLZ* 79 (1954) 577-592. Eng. trans.: *The Lord's Supper According to the New Testament*. Trans. J. M. Davis. Philadelphia: 1967.

0808 Higgins, A. J. B. "The Origins of the Eucharist," *NTS* 1 (1954-55) 200-209.

0809 Emerton, J. A. "The Aramaic Underlying *to haima mou tēs diathēkēs* in Mk. xiv.24," *JTS* 6 (1955) 238-240.

0810 Foerster, W. "Lukas 22,31f," *ZNW* 46 (1955) 129-133.

0811 Günter, J. "Das Becherwort Jesu," *TGl* 45 (1955) 47-49.

0812 Leenhardt, F. J. " 'Ceci est mon corps.' Explication des paroles de Jésus-Christ," *Cahiers Theologiques de L'Actualité Protestante* 37 (1955) 1-75.

0813 Oepke, A. "Kann die Auslegung der Abendmahlstexte des Neuen Testaments für das Abendmahlsgespräch der Kirche hilfreich sein?" *TLZ* 80 (1955) 129-142.

0814 Schürmann, H. "Die Gestalt der urchristlichen Eucharistiefeier," *MTZ* 6 (1955) 107-122.

0815 Benoit, P. "The Holy Eucharist I," *Scr* 7 (1956) 97-108.

0816 Burkill, T. A. "The Last Supper," *Numen* 3 (1956) 161-177.

0817 Taylor, V. "Review of *Der Paschamahlbericht,* by H. Schürmann," *NTS* 2 (1956) 207-209.

0818 Sparks, H. F. D. "St Luke's Transpositions," *NTS* 3 (1956-57) 219-223.

0819 Benoit, P. "Les récits de l'institution et leur portée," *LumVit* 31 (1957) 49-76.

0820 Chadwick, H. "The Shorter Text of Luke xxii.15-20," *HTR* 50 (1957) 249-258.

0821 Christensen, J. "Le fils de l'homme s'en va, ainsi qu'il est écrit de lui," *ST* 10 (1957) 28-39.

0822 Turner, N. "The Style of St. Mark's Eucharistic Words," *JTS* 8 (1957) 108-111.

0823 Dupont, J. " 'Ceci est mon corps,' 'Ceci est mon sang,' " *NRT* 80 (1958) 1025-1041.

0824 Taylor, V. "Review of *Der Einsetzungsbericht* and *Jesu Abschiedsrede*, by H. Schürmann," *NTS* 4 (1958) 223-225.

0825 duRoy, J. B. "Le dernier repas de Jésus," *BVC* 26 (1959) 44-52.

0826 Fransen, I. "Le Baptême de Sang (Luc 22,1-23)," *BVC* 25 (1959) 20-28.

0827 Steinbeck, J. "Das Abendmahl Jesu unter Berücksichtigung moderner Forschung," *Numen* 6 (1959) 51-60.

0828 Taylor, V. "The New Testament Origins of Holy Communion," *London Quarterly and Holborn Review* 28 (1959) 84-90.

0829 Sykes, M. H. "The Eucharist as 'Anamnesis'," *ExpT* 71 (1959-60) 115-118.

0830 Cooke, B. "Synoptic Presentation of the Eucharist as Covenant Sacrifice," *TS* 21 (1960) 1-44.

0831 Gottlieb, H. *"TO HAIMA MOY TĒS DIATHĒKĒS,"* *ST* 14 (1960) 115-118.

0832 Knoch, G. "Ursprüngliche Gestalt und wesentlicher Gehalt der neutestamentlichen Abendmahlsberichte," *BK* 15 (1960) 37-40.

0833 Kosmala, H. " 'Das tut zu meinen Gedächtnis'," *NovT* 4 (1960) 81-94.

0834 Stuhlmueller, C. "The Holy Eucharist: Symbol of the Psssion," *Worship* 34 (1960) 195-205.

0835 Ahern, B. M. "Gathering the Fragments: The Lord's Supper," *Worship* 35 (1961) 424-429.

0836 Temple, S. "The Two traditions of the Last Supper, Betrayal and Arrest," *NTS* 7 (1960-61) 77-85.

0837 Kugelmann, R. "This Is My Blood of the New Covenant," *Worship* 35 (1961) 421-424.

0838 Rost, L. "Zwei Glossen zum Sinn des Abendmahls," *ThViat* 8 (1961-62) 227-231.

0839 Daube, D. "Death as Release in the Bible," *NovT* 5 (1962) 94-98.

0840 Cooper, J. C. "Problem of the Text in Luke 22:19-20," *LQ* 14 (1962) 39-48.

0841 Emerton, J. A. "*To haima mou tēs diathēkēs*. The Evidence of the Syriac Versions," *JTS* 13 (1962) 111-117.

0842 Le Deaut, R. "Goûter le calice de la mort," *Bib* 43 (1962) 82-86.

0843 Mueller, J. T. " 'My Blood of the Covenant'—The Evidence of the Syriac Versions," *CTM* 33 (1962) 675.

0844 Aalen, S. "Das Abendmahl als Opfermahl im Neuen Testament," *NovT* 6 (1963) 128-152.

0845 Adam, A. "Ein vergessener Aspekt des frühchristlichen Herrenmahles," *TLZ* 88 (1963) 9-20.

0846 Fuller, R. H. "The Double Origin of the Eucharist," *BR* 8 (1963) 60-72.

0847 Priest, J. F. "The Messiah and the Meal in IQSa," *JBL* 82 (1963) 95-100.

0848 Coppens, J. "L'eucharistie, sacrement et sacrifice de la nouvelle Alliance, fondement de l'Église," *Aux origines de l'Église. Recherches Bibliques*. Bruges/Paris: 1964, 125-152.

0849 Dupont, J. "Le Logion des douze trônes (Mt. 19,28; Lc. 22, 28-30)," *Bib* 45 (1964) 355-392. = *Études sur les Évangile synoptiques*. Leuven: 1985, 2:706-743.

0850 Emerton, J. A. "Mark xiv.24 and the Targum to the Psalter," *JTS* 15 (1964) 58-59.

0851 Robinson, D. W. B. "The Eucharistic Sacrifice in the Sacrament of the Body and Blood of Christ," *Reformed Theological Review* 23 (1964) 65-74.

0852 Coppens, J. "Miscellanées blibliques. XXXIV. L'eucharistie dans le Nouveau Testament," *ETL* 41 (1965) 142-147.

0853 Braumann, G. "Mit euch, Mth. 26,29," *TZ* 21 (1965) 161-169.

0854 Fensham, F. C. "Judas' Hand in the Bowl and Qumran," *RevQ* 18 (1965) 259-261.

0855 Lash, N. "The Eucharist: Sacrifice or Meal," *ClerRev* 50 (1965) 907-922.

0856 Power, J. "Pasch and Easter," *Furrow* 16 (1965) 195-204.

0857 Braun, H. "Das Herrenmahl," *Qumran und das Neue Testament*. Tübingen: 1966, 229-54.

0858 Emery, P.-Y. "L'Eucharistie: sacrifice du Christ et de l'Église (note conjointe)," *VCaro* 20 (1966) 65-72.

0859 Caird, G. B. "The Last Supper," *ExpT* 78 (1966) 58.

0860 Seemann, M. "La catèchése sur l'eucharistie dans une perspective biblique et oecumenique," *VCaro* 20 (1966) 50-64.

0861 David, J. E. "*To haima mou tēs diathēkēs*: Mt. 26:28, Un faux problème," *Bib* 48 (1967) 291-292.

0862 Feuillet, A. "Le logion sur la rancon," *RSPT* 51 (1967) 365-402.

0863 Hahn, F. "Die alttestamentlichen Motive in der urchristlichen Abendmahlsüberlieferung," *EvT* 27 (1967) 337-374.

0864 Leaney, A. R. C. "What was the Lord's Supper?" *Theology* 70 (1967) 51-62.

0865 Most, W. G. "A Biblical Theology of Redemption in a Covenant Framework," *CBQ* 29 (1967) 1-19.

0866 Coppens, J. "L'Eucharistie Neotestamentaire," *Exégèse et Théologie*. Ed. G. Thils and R. E. Brown. BETL 26. Gembloux/Paris: 1968, 262-281.

0867 Gese, H. "Psalm 22 und das Neue Testament. Der älteste Bericht vom Tode Jesu und die Entstehung des Herrenmahles," *ZTK* 65 (1968) 1-22.

0868 Smith, M. A. "The Influence of the Liturgies on the New Testament Text of the Last Supper Narratives," *SE* V (TU 103 1968) 207-218.

0869 Soltmann, M. L. " 'Solches tut zu meinem Gadächtnis . . .' Das heilige Abendmahl, die Sederfeier Jesu," *Israel Forum* 10 (1968) 13-17.

0870 Vööbus, A. "A New Approach to the Problem of the Shorter and Longer Text in Luke," *NTS* 15 (1968-69) 457-463.

0871 Kilmartin, E. "The Last Supper and the Earliest Eucharists of the Church," *The Breaking of Bread*. Ed. P. Benoit et.al. Concilium 40. New York: 1969, 35-47.

0872 Lussier, E. "Some reflections on the Narrative of the Institution of the Eucharist," *Chicago Studies* 8 (1969) 249-259.

0873 Schürmann, H. "Jesus' Words in the Light of His Actions at the Last Supper," *The Breaking of Bread*. Ed. P. Benoit et.al. Concilium 40. New York: 1969, 119-131.

0874 Stagg, F. "The Lord's Supper in the New Testament," *RevExp* 66 (1969) 5-14.

0875 Beck, N. A. "The Last Supper as an Efficacious Symbolic Act," *JBL* 89 (1970) 192-198.

0876 Descamps, A. "Les origines de l'Eucharistie," *Responses chrétiennes* 12 (1970) 57-125. = *Jésus et L'Église*. Leuven: 1987, 455-496.

0877 Ligier, L. "From the Last Supper to the Eucharist," *The New Liturgy*. Ed. L. D. Shepherd. London: 1970, 113-125.

0878 Lys, D. "Mon corps, c'est ceci (Notule sur Mt 26/26-28 et par.)," *ETR* 45 (1970) 389.

0879 Minear, P. S. "Some Glimpses of Luke's Sacramental Theology," *Worship* 44 (1970) 322-331.

0880 Schürmann, H. "Der Abendsmahlsbericht Lukas 22,7-38 als Gottesdienstordnung, Gemeindeordnung, Lebensordnung," *Ursprung und Gestalt*. Düsseldorf: 1970, 108-150.

0881 Schürmann, H. "Das apostolische Interesse am eucharistischen Kelch," *Ursprung und Gestalt*. Düsseldorf: 1970, 188-198.

0882 Schürmann, H. "Jesus Abendmahlsworte im Lichte seiner Abendmahlshandlung," *Ursprung und Gestalt*. Düsseldorf: 1970, 100-107.

0883 Vööbus, A. "Kritische Beobachtung über die lukanische Darstellung des Herrenmahls," *ZNW* 62 (1970) 102-110.

0884 Hein, K. "Judas Iscariot. Key to the Last Supper Narratives?" *NTS* 17 (1970-71) 227-232.

0885 Crespy, G. "Recherche sur la signification politique de la mort due Christ," *Lumière et Vie* 20 (1971) 89-109.

0886 Didier, J. D. "A l'institution de l'Eucharistie, le Christ a-t-il dit: 'Ce Sang est verse?' ou 'sera verse'?" *Espirit et Vie* 81 (1971) 564-565.

0887 Irwin, K. W. "The Supper Text in the Gospel of Saint Matthew," *DunRev* 11 (1971) 170-184.

0888 Loewe, H. "Die doppelte Wurzel des Abendmahles in Jesu Tischgemeinschaft," *Abendmahl in der Tischgemeinschaft*. Ed. H. Loewe. Kassel: 1971, 9-22.

0889 Nussbaum, O. "Die Eucharistiefeier als Anamnese (Opfer und Mahl)," *BLit* 44 (1971) 2-16.

0890 Patsch, H. "Abendmahlsterminologie ausserhalb der Einsetzungs-berichte. Erwägungen zur Traditionsgeschichte der Abendmahl-sworte," *ZNW* 61 (1971) 210-231.

0891 Crossan, J. D. "Redaction and Citation in Mark 11:9-10, 17 and 14:27," SBLASP (1972) 1:17-61.

0892 Jeremias, J. " 'This is my body . . .'," *ExpT* 83 (1972) 196-203.

0893 Kertelge, K. "Die urchristliche Abendmahlsüberlieferung und der historische Jesus," *TTZ* 81 (1972) 193-202.

0894 Pigulla, W. "Das für viele vergossene Blut," *MTZ* 23 (1972) 72-82.

0895 Frankemölle, H. "26,29: Die Gemeinde—mit Christus beim escha-tologischen Mahl"; "26,38.40: Die Nachfolge der Jünger im Leiden," *Jahwebund und Kirche Christi*. NTABh 10. Münster: 1973, 37-42

0896 Ziesler, J. A. "The Vow of Abstinence: A Note on Mark 14,25 parr.," *Colloquium* 5 (1972) 12-14; 6 (1973) 49-50.

0897 Bammel, E. "P 64 (67) and the Last Supper," *JTS* 24 (1973) 189.

0898 Bayer, O. "Tod Gottes und Herrenmahl," *ZTK* 70 (1973) 346-363.

0899 Flusser, D. "The Last Supper and the Essenes," *Immanuel* 2 (1973) 23-27.

0900 Léon-Dufour, X. "Das letzte Abendmahl: Stiftung und kultische Aktualisierung," *BLit* 46 (1973) 167-177.

0901 Leroy, H. " 'Mein Blut . . . zur Vergebung den Sunden' (Mt. 26, 28). Zur matthäischen Interpretation des Abendmahles," *Das Evangelium auf dem Weg zum Menschen*. Ed. O. Knoch, F. Messerschmid and A. Zenner (Fest. H. Kahlefeld). Frankfurt: 1973, 43-54.

0902 Palmer, D. "Defining a Vow of Abstinence," *Colloquium* 6 (1973) 38-41.

0903 Reid, W. S. "The Death of Christ: Historical and Contempora-neous," *EvQ* 45 (1973) 69-80.

0904 Smith, M. A. "The Lucan Last Supper Narrative," *SE* VI (TU 112 1973) 502-509.

0905 Synge, F. S. "Mark 14:18-25. Supper and Rite," *JTSAfric* 4 (1973) 38-43.

0906 Ziesler, J. A. "The Vow of Abstinence Again," *Colloquium* 6 (1973) 49-50.

0907 Grassi, J. A. "The Eucharist in the Gospel of Mark," *AEF* 168 (1974) 595-608.

0908 Kilpatrick, G. D. "Eucharist as Sacrifice and Sacrament in the New Testament," *Neues Testament und Kirche*. Ed. J. Gnilka (Fest. R. Schnackenburg). Freiburg: 1974, 429-433.

0909 LaVerdiere, E. A. "A Discourse at the Last Supper," *TBT* 71 (1974) 1540-1548.

0910 Hahn, F. "Zum Stand der Erforschung des urchristlichen Herrenmahls," *EvT* 35 (1975) 533-563.

0911 Léon-Dufour, X. "Jésus devant sa mort, à la lumière des textes de l'institution eucharistique et des discours d'adieu," *Jésus aux origines de la christologie*. Ed. J. Dupont. BETL 40. Leuven/ Gembloux: 1975, 141-168.

0912 Schroeder, R. P. "The Worthless Shepherd. A Study of Mk. 14,27," *CurTM* 2 (1975) 342-344.

0913 Wagner, V. "Der Bedeutungswandel von *berit hadasa* bei der Ausgestaltung der Abendmahlsworte," *EvT* 35 (1975) 538-544.

0914 Rese, M. "Zur Problematik von Kurz— und Langtext in Luk. XXII.17ff," *NTS* 22 (1975-76) 15-31.

0915 Pesch, R. "Das Abendmahl und Jesu Todesverständnis," *Der Tod Jesu*. Ed. K. Kertelge. Freiburg: 1976, 137-187.

0916 Robbins, V. K. "Last Meal: Preparation, Betrayal, and Absence," *The Passion in Mark: Studies on Mark 14-16*. Ed. W. H. Kelber. Philadelphia: 1976, 21-38.

0917 Schelkle, K. H. "Das Herrenmahl," *Rechtfertigung*. Ed. J. Friedrich, W. Pöhlmann, and P. Stuhlmacher. (Fest. E. Käsemann). Tübingen: 1976, 385-402.

0918 Schneider, G. "Du aber stärke deine Brüder! (Lk. 22,32). Die Aufgabe des Petrus nach Lukas," *Catholica* 30 (1976) 200-206.

0919 Léon-Dufour, X. " 'Faites ceci en mémoire de moi.' Luc. 22,19 -1 Corinthiens 11,25," *Christus* 24 (1977) 200-208.

0920 Merklein, H. "Erwägungen zur Überlieferungsgeschichte der neutestamentlichen Abendmahlstraditionen," *BZ* 21 (1977) 88-101; 235-244.

0921 Pesch, R. "The Last Supper and Jesus' Understanding of His Death," *Bible Bhashyam* 3 (1977) 58-75.

0922 Rickards, R. R. "Luke 22.25—They are called 'Friends of the People'," *BT* 28 (1977) 445-446.

0923 Winnett, A. R. "The Breaking of Bread: Does it Symbolize the Passion?" *ExpT* 88 (1977) 181-182.

0924 Edanad, A. "Institution of the Eucharist according to the Synoptic Gospels," *Bibel Bhashyam* 4 (1978) 322-332.

0925 Descamps, A. "Cénacle et Calvaire. Les Vues de H. Schürmann," *RTL* 10 (1979) 335-347. = *Jésus et L'Église*. Leuven: 1987, 497-509.

0926 Ellington, J. "The Translation of *hymneō* 'sing a hymn' in Mark 14:26 and Matthew 26:30," *BT* 30 (1979) 445-446.

0927 Gregg, D. W. A. "Hebraic Antecedents to the *Anamnesis* Formula," *TynBul* 20 (1979) 165-168.

0928 Kertelge, K. "Abendmahlsgemeinschaft und Kirchengemeinschaft im Neuen Testament und in der Alten Kirche," *Einheit der Kirche. Grundlegung im Neuen Testament*. QD 84. Freiburg/Basel/Vienna: 1979, 94-132.

0929 Bauer, J. B. "Fragen zur revidierten Einheitsübersetzung (III) 'Die Vielen', das sind 'alle' (Mk. 14,24)," *BuL* 53 (1980) 137-139.

0930 Cousin, H. "Dier a-t-il sacrifié son fils Jésus?" *Lumière et Vie* 29 (1980) 55-67.

0931 Emminghaus, J. H. "Stammen die Einsetzungsworte der Eucharistie von Jesus selber?" *BuL* 53 (1980) 36-38.

0932 Hahn, F. "Das Abendmahl und Jesu Todesverständnis," *TR* 76 (1980) 265-272. = *Exegetische Beiträge zum ökumenischen Gespräch. Gesammelte Aufsätze*. Göttingen: 1986, 1: 253-261.

0933 Kertelge, K. "Das Abendmahl Jesu im Markusevangelium," *Begegnung mit dem Wort*. Ed. J. Zmijewski and E. Nellessen (Fest. H. Zimmermann). BBB 53. Bonn: 1980, 67-80.

0934 Ruckstuhl, E. "Neue und alte Überlegungen zu den Abendmahlsworten Jesu," *SNTU* 5 (1980) 79-106.

0935 Reumann, J. H. "The Problem of the Lord's Supper as Matrix for Albert Schweitzer's 'Quest of the Historical Jesus'," *NTS* 27 (1980-81) 475-487.

0936 Amphoux, C. B. "Le dernier repas de Jésus. Lc 22,15-20 par," *ETR* 56 (1981) 449-454.

0937 Blank, J. "Der 'eschatologische Ausblick' Mk 14,25 und seine Bedeuting," *Kontinuität und Einheit* (Fest. F. Mussner). Freiburg/Basel/Vienna: 1981, 500-518.

0938 Daly, R. J. "The Eucharist and Redemption: The Last Supper and Jesus' Understanding of His Death," *BTB* 11 (1981) 21-27.

0939 Guillet, J. "Luc 22,29. Une formule johannique dans l'évangile de Luc," *RSR* 69 (1981) 113-122.

0940 Léon-Dufour, X. "Das letzte Mahl Jesu und die testamentarische Tradition nach Lk 22," *ZKT* 103 (1981) 33-55.

0941 Weren, W. "The Lord's Supper: An Inquiry into the Coherence in Lk 22,14-18," *Fides Sacramenti*. Ed. H. J. Auf der Maur (Fest. P. Smulders). Assen: 1981, 9-26.

0942 Huser, T. "Les récits de l'institution de la Céne. Dissemblances et traditions," *Hokhma* 21 (1982) 28-50.

0943 Johnson, P. F. "A Suggested Understanding of the Eucharistic Words," *SE* VII (TU 126, 1982) 265-270.

0944 Léon-Dufour, X. "'Prenez! Ceci est mon corps pour vous,' " *NRT* 104 (1982) 223-240.

0945 Magne, J. M. "Les paroles sur la coupe," *Logia. Les paroles de Jésus—The Sayings of Jesus. Memorial Joseph Coppens*. BETL 59. Leuven: 1982, 485-490.

0946 Schlosser, J. "La genèse de Luc, XXII, 25-27," *RB* 89 (1982) 52-70.

0947 Senior, D. P. "The Eucharist in Mark: Mission, Reconciliation, Hope," *BTB* 12 (1982) 67-72.

0948 van Iersel, B. " 'To Galilee' or 'in Galilee' in Mark 14,28 and 16,7?" *ETL* 58 (1982) 365-370.

0949 Achtemeier, P. "It's the Little Things that Count (Mark 14:17-21; Luke 4:1-13; Matthew 18:1-4)," *BA* 46 (1983) 30-31.

0950 Knoch, O. " 'Tut das zu meinem Gedächtnis!' (Lk 22,30; 1 Kor. 11,24f). Die Feier der Eucharistie in den urchristlichen Gemeinden," *Freude am Gottesdienst*. Ed. J. Schreiner (Fest. O. Plöger). Stuttgart: 1983, 31-42.

0951 Pesch, R. "Das Evangelium in Jerusalem: 'Mk. 14,12-26 als älteste Überlieferungsgut der Urgemeinde'," *Das Evangelium und die Evangelien*. Ed. P. Stuhlmacher. Tübingen: 1983, 113-155.

0952 Rasmussen, L. "Luke 22:24-27," *Int* 37 (1983) 73-76.

0953 Schwank, B. " 'Das ist mein Leib, der für euch hingegeben wird' (Lk 22,19)," *Erbe und Auftrag* 59 (1983) 279-290.

0954 Sweetland, D. M. "The Lord's Supper and the Lukan Community," *BTB* 13 (1983) 23-27.

0955 Arnott, A. G. " 'The first day of unleavened . . .' Mt. 26.17, Mk. 14.12, Lk. 22.7," *BT* 35 (1984) 235-238.

0956 Balembo, B. "Le produit de la vigne et le vin nouveau. Analyse exégétique de Mc 14,25," *RAT* 8 (1984) 5-16.

0957 Hagemeyer, O. " 'Tut dies zu meinem Gedächtnis' (1Kor 11,24f.; Lk 22,19)," *Praesentia Christi*. Ed. L. Lies (Fest. J. Betz). Düsseldorf: 1984, 110-117.

0958 LaVerdiere, E. A. "Do this in Remembrance of Me," *Emmanuel* 90 (1984) 365-369.

0959 Petzer, J. H. "Luke 22:19b-20 and the Structure of the Passage," *NovT* 26 (1984) 249-252.

0960 Wojciechowski, M. "Le nazireat et la Passion (Mc 14,25a; 15,23)," *Bib* 65 (1984) 94-96.

0961 Wilkens, H. "Die Anfange des Herrenmahls," *Jahrbuch für Liturgie und Hymnologie* 28 (1984) 55-65.

0962 Carl, W. J. III. "Mark 14:22-25," *Int* 39 (1985) 296-301.

0963 Derrett, J. D. M. "The Upper Room and the Dish," *HeyJ* 26 (1985) 373-382.

0964 Kurz, W. S. "Luke 22:14-38 and Greco-Roman and Biblical Farewell Addresses," *JBL* 104 (1985) 251-268.

0965 O'Toole, R. F. "What's the Lord's Supper Can Mean for Religious," *RevRel* 44 (1985) 237-249.

0966 Jones, R. C. "The Lord's Supper and the Concept of Anamnesis," *Word and World* 6 (1986) 434-445.

0967 Laurance, J. D. "The Eucharist as the Imitation of Christ," *TS* 47 (1986) 286-296.

0968 Lull, D. J. "The Servant-Benefactor as a Model of Greatness (Luke 22:24-30)," *NovT* 28 (1986) 289-305.

0969 Quesnell, Q. "The Women at Luke's Supper," *Political Issues in Luke-Acts*. Ed. R. J. Cassidy and P. Scharper. Maryknoll: 1983, 59-79.

0970 Burchard, C. "The Importance of Joseph and Asenath for the Study of the New Testament: A General Survey and a Fresh Look at the Lord's Supper," *NTS* 33 (1987) 102-134.

0971 Green, J. B. "Preparation for Passover (Luke 22:7-13): A Question of Redactional Technique," *NovT* 29 (1987) 305-319.

0972 Lindars, B. "*Joseph and Asenath* and the Eucharist," *Scripture: Meaning and Method*. Ed. B. P. Thompson (Fest. A. T. Hanson). Hull: 1987, 181-199.

0973 Neirynck, F. "*TIS ESTIN O PAISAS SE*. Mt 26,68/Lk 22,64 (diff. Mk 14,65)," *ETL* 63 (1987) 5-47.

0974 Selew, P. "The Last Supper Discourse in Luke 22/21-38," *Forum* 3 (1987) 70-95.

0975 Macina, M. "Fonction liturgique et eschatologique de l'anamnese eucharistique (Lc 22,19; 1 Co 11, 24.25). Réexamen de la question à la lumière des Écritures et des sources juives," *Ephemerides Liturgicae* 102 (1988) 3-25.

See also 0001, 0138, 0341, 0349, 0370, 0382, 0384, 0429, 0456, 0632-0668, 0976-0990

XI. The Saying About the Two Swords

Articles

0976 Wright, A. "Study of St. Luke xxii. 35-38," *ExpT* (1892-93) 153-157.

0977 Schlatter, A. "Die beiden Schwerter Lk. 22.35-38," *BFCT* 20 (1916) 4-75.

0978 Hobhouse, S. " 'And he that hath no sword, let him . . . buy one' (Luke xxii.35-38)," *ExpT* 30 (1918-19) 278-279.

0979 Napier, T. M. "The Enigma of the Swords," *ExpT* 49 (1937-38) 467-470.

0980 Finlayson, S. K. "The Enigma of the Swords," *ExpT* 50 (1938-39) 563.

0981 Western, W. "The Enigma of the Swords," *ExpT* 50 (1938-39) 377.

0982 Napier, T. M. "The Enigma of the Swords (Luke xxii.35-38)," *ExpT* 51 (1939-40) 204.

0983 Western, W. "The Enigma of the Swords (Luke xxii.38)," *ExpT* 52 (1940-41) 357.

0984 Hall, S. G. "Swords of Offence," *SE* I (TU 73 1959) 499-502.

0985 Minear, P. S. "A Note on Luke xxii.36," *NovT* 7 (1964) 128-134.

0986 Bartsch, H. W. "Jesu Schwertwort, Lukas xxii.35-38: Überlieferungsgeschichtliche Studien," *NTS* 20 (1973-74) 190-203.

0987 Schwarz, G. "*Kyrie, idou machairai hōde dyo* (Lc. 22,35-38)," *Biblischen Notizen* 8 (1979), 22.

0988 Derrett, J. D. M. "History and the Two Swords," *Studies in the New Testament*. Leiden: 1982, 3:200-214.

0989 Gillman, J. "A Temptation to Violence: The Two Swords in Lk 22:35-38," *LS* 9 (1982) 142-153.

0990 Lampe, G. W. H. "The two swords," *Jesus and the Politics of His Day*. Ed. E. Bammel and C. F. D. Moule. Cambridge: 1984, 335-352

See also 0764, 0765, 0880, 0964

XII. Gethsemene

Books

0991 Tindall, P. N. *Gethsemane: The Passion of Jesus.* London: 1941.

0992 Lövestam, E. *Spiritual Wakefulness in the New Testament.* Lund: 1963.

0993 Marchel, W. *Abba, Père! La prière du Christ et des Chrétiens. Etude exégétique sur les origines et las signification de l'invocation à la divinité comme père, avant et dans le Nouveau Testament.* AB 19. Rome: 1971.

0994 Holleran, J. W. *The Synoptic Gethsemane: A Critical Study.* Analecta Gregoriana 191. Rome: 1973.

0995 Feuillet, A. *L'Agonie de Gethsémani: enquête exégétique et théologique.* Paris, 1977.

0996 Stanley, D. M. *Jesus in Gethsemane: The Early Church Reflects on the Suffering of Jesus.* New York: Paulist Press, 1980.

0997 Feldmeier, R. *Die Krisis des Gottessohnes. Die Gethsemaneerzählung als Schlüssel des Markuspassion.* WUNT 2/21. Tübingen: 1987.

Articles

0998 Chase, T. "*To loipon.* Matt. xxvi.45," *JBL* 6 (1886) 131-135.

0999 Gilbert, J. "The Agony in the Garden," *Exp* 3d ser. 5 (1887) 180-193.

1000 Bernard, J. H. "St. Mark xiv. 41-42," *ExpT* 3 (1891-92) 451-453.

1001 Kurrikoff, A. "Christus in Gethsemane," *MNEKR* 24 (1891) 23-34.

1002 Petavel, E. "The House of Gethsemane," *Exp* 4th ser. 3 (1891) 220-232.

1003 Keen, W. W. "The Bloody Sweat of our Lord," *BQR* 14 (1892) 169-175.

1004 Schwartz, J. W. "Jesus in Gethsemane," *LQ* 22 (1892) 267-271.

1005 Robson, J. "The Meaning of Christ's Prayer in Gethsemane," *ExpT* 6 (1894-95) 522-523.

1006 Stooke-Vaughn, F. S. "Sit Ye here," *ExpT* 6 (1894-95) 94-95.

1007 Aars, J. "Zu Matth. 26,45 und Marc, 14,41" *ZWT* 38 (1895) 378-383.

1008 Alexander, W. M.; Cunningham, J. G.; Watt, D. G.; and Milne, G. "The Meaning of Christ's Prayer in Gethsemane," *ExpT* 7 (1895-96) 34-38.

1009 West, T.; Whyte, J.; Reith, J.; Little, J. A. S.; and Grant, I. "The Meaning of Christ's Prayer in Gethsemane," *ExpT* 7 (1895-96) 118-121.

1010 McMichael, E. F.; Ross, J.; and Wallis, R. E. "Our Lord's Prayer in Gethsemane," *ExpT* 7 (1895-96) 502-505.

1011 Keen, W. W. "Further Studies on the Bloody Sweat of our Lord," *BSac* 54 (1897) 469-483.

1012 Arthus, M. and Chanson, V. "Les sueurs de sang," *RT* 6 (1898) 673-696.

1013 Malan, C. "La crainte que ressent le seigneur Jésus à l'approche de la mort," *RTP* 31 (1898) 439-452.

1014 Harnack, A. "Probleme im Texte der Leidensgeschichte Jesu," *SAB* (Berlin: 1901) 251-266.

1015 Smith, H. "Acts xx.8 and Luke xxii.43," *ExpT* 16 (1904-05) 478.

1016 De Zwaan, J. "The Text and Exegesis of Mark xiv.41, and the Papyri," *Exp* 6th ser. 12 (1905) 459-472.

1017 Zeydner, H. "*Apechei,* Mark XIV:41," *TS* 43 (1905) 439-442.

1018 Thomson, A. E. "The Gethsemane Agony," *BSac* 67 (1910) 598-610.

1019 Clarke, W. K. L. "St. Luke and Pseudepigrapha: Two Parallels," *JTS* 15 (1914) 597-599.

1020 Moffatt, J. "Exegetica.—Luke xxii.44," *Exp* (1914) 90-92.

1021 Lotz, W. "Das Sinnbild des Bechers," *NKZ* 28 (1917) 396-407.

1022 Gibson, J. M. "The Gethsemane of the Fourth Gospel," *ExpT* 30 (1918-19) 76-79.

1023 Baldwin, E. St. G. "Gethsemane: the fulfillment of prophecy," *BSac* 77 (1920) 429-436.

1024 Coburn, C. M. "Gethsemane," *Biblical World* 54 (1920) 139-141.

1025 Wilson, W. E. "Our Lord's Agony in the Garden," *ExpT* 32 (1920-21) 549-551.

1026 Lebreton, J. "L'Agonie de Notre-Seigneur," *RA* 33 (1921-22) 705-725; 34 (1922) 9-22.

1027 Starkie, W. J. M. "Gospel according to St. Matthew xxvi.45 and xxviii.2," *Hermathena* 19 (1922) 141-143.

1028 Holzmeister, U. "Spricht Epiphanius (Ancoratus 31,4) vom Blutschweiss des Herrn oder von seinen Tränen?" *ZTK* 47 (1923) 309-314.

1029 Vail, A. L. "Gethsemane," *RevExp* 20 (1923) 188-200.

1030 Glorieux, P. "Le mysterè de l'agonie," *VS* 19 (1928-29) 601-641.

1031 Smisson, E. A. "Mark xiv.41: *Apechei*," *ExpT* 40 (1928-29) 528.

1032 Bonnetain, P. "La cause de l'agonie de Jésus," *RS* 50 (1930) 681-690.

1033 Fiebig, P. "Jesu Gebet in Gethsemane," *Der Geisteskampf der Gegenwart* 66 (1930) 121-125.

1034 Petitot, H. "L'agonie de Jésus," *VS* 22 (1930) 238-256; 23 (1930) 24-40.

1035 Bonnetain, P. "La crainte de la mort en Jésus agonisant," *RA* 53 (1931) 276-295.

1036 Brun, L. "Engel und Blutschweiss Lc. 22:43-44," *ZNW* 32 (1933) 265-276.

1037 Barth, K. "Kirche gestern, heute, morgen," *EvT* 1 (1934-35) 289-295.

1038 Hudson, J. T. "Irony in Gethsemane?" *ExpT* 46 (1934-35 383.

1039 Bate, H. N. "Luke xxii 40," *JTS* 36 (1935) 76-77.

1040 Heitmüller, F. "Gethsemane," *Jesu Dienst* 17 (1938) 314-318.

1041 Joüon, P. "Marc 14,31," *RSR* 29 (1939) 240-241.

1042 Thomson, A. E. "Our Lord's Prayer in the Garden," *BSac* 97 (1940) 110-116.

1043 Bishop, E. F. F. "A Stones Throw," *ExpT* 53 (1941-42) 270-271.

1044 Black, M. "The Cup Metaphor in Mark 14:36," *ExpT* 59 (1947-48) 195.

1045 Cranfield, C. E. B. "The Cup Metaphor in Mark 14:36 and Parallels," *ExpT* 59 (1947-48) 137-138.

1046 Lightfoot, R. H. "A consideration of three passages in St. Mark's Gospel," *In Memoriam Ernst Lohmeyer*. Ed. W. Schmauch. Stuttgart: 1951, 110-115.

1047 Kuhn, K. G. "*Peirasmos—hamartia—sarx* im Neuen Testament und die damit zusammenhängende Vorstellung," *ZTK* 49 (1952) 200-222.

1048 Schürmann, H. "Lk. 22,42a das älteste Zeugnis für Lk. 22,20," *MTZ* 3 (1952) 185-188. = *Traditionsgeschichtliche Untersuchung zu den Synoptischen Evangelien*. Düsseldorf: 1968, 193-197.

1049 Kuhn, K. G. "Jesus in Gethsemene," *EvT* 12 (1952-53) 260-285.

1050 Dibelius, M. "Gethsemane," *Crozer Quarterly* 12 (1953) 254-265.

1051 McCasland, S. V. "Abba, Father," *JBL* 72 (1953) 79-91.

1052 Aschermann, H. "Zum Agoniegebet Jesu Lc XXII,43 sq.," *ThViat* 5 (1953-54) 143-173.

1053 Evans, C. F. " 'I will go before you into Galilee'," *JTS* 5 (1954) 3-18.

1054 Strobel, A. "Die Psalmengrundlage der Gethsemane—Parallel Hbr, V,7ff," *ZNW* 45 (1954) 252-266.

1055 Daube, D. "The Sleeping Companions," *The New Testament and Rabbinic Judaism*. London: 1956, 332-335.

1056 Indemans, J. H. H. A. "Das Lukas-Evangelium XXII,45," *SO* 32 (1956) 81-83.

1057 Kenny, A. "The Transfiguration and the Agony in the Garden," *CBQ* 19 (1957) 444-452.

1058 Curtis, J. B. "An Investigation of the Mount of Olives in the Judeo-Christian Tradition," *HUCA* 28 (1957) 137-180.

1059 Kuhn, K. G. "New Light on Temptation, Sin and Flesh in the New Testament," *The Scrolls and the New Testament*. Ed. K. Stendahl. New York: 1957, 94-113.

1060 Schmauch, W. "Der Ölberg," *TLZ* 7 (1957) 391-397.

1061 Daube, D. "A Prayer Pattern in Judaism," *SE* 1 (TU 73 1959) 539-545.

1062 Hering, R. "Simples remarques sur la prière à Gethsémane. Matthieu 26,36-46; Marc 14,32-42; Luc 22,40-46," *RHPR* 39 (1959) 97-102.

1063 Brown, R. E. "Incidents that are Units in the Synoptic Gospels but Dispersed in St. John," *CBQ* 23 (1961) 143-160.

1064 Hering, J. "Zwei exegetische Probleme in der Perikope von Jesus in Gethsemane (Mk. 14,32-42 parr.)," *Neotestamentica et Patristica* (Fest. O. Cullmann). NovTSup 6. Leiden: 1962, 64-69.

1065 Birdsall, J. N. "*Egrēgoreō*," *JTS* 14 (1963) 390-391.

1066 Boman, T. "Der Gebetskampf Jesu," *NTS* 10 (1963-64) 261-273.

1067 Armbruster, J. C. "The Messianic Significance of the Agony in the Garden," *Scr* 16 (1964) 111-119.

1068 Trémel, Y. B. "L'agonie du Christ," *LumVit* 68 (1964) 79-104.

1069 Wulf, F. " 'Der Geist ist willig, das Fleisch schwach' (Mk. 14, 38)," *GuL* 37 (1964) 241-243.

1070 Braumann, G. "Leidenskelch und Todestaufe," *ZNW* 56 (1965) 178-183.

1071 Dautzenbuerg, G. "*Psyche* in Mk 14,34/Mt 26,38 und Jo 12,27," *Sein Leben bewahren*. STANT 14. Munich: 1966, 127-133.

1072 Lescow, T. "Jesus in Gethsemane," *EvT* 26 (1966) 141-159.

1073 Pelcé, F. "Jésus à Gethsémani. Remarques comparatives sur les trois récits évangéliques," *Foi et Vie* 65 (1966) 89-99.

1074 Robinson, B. P. "Gethsemane: The Synoptic and Johannine Viewpoints," *CQR* 167 (1966) 4-11.

1075 Johnson, S. L., Jr. "The Agony of Christ," *BSac* 124 (1967) 303-313.

1076 Lescow, T. "Jesus in Gethsemane bei Lukas und im Hebräerbrief," *ZNW* 58 (1967) 215-239.

1077 Bobichon, M. "L'agonie, tentation du Seigneur," *BTS 99 (1968) 2-5*.

1078 Brongers, H. A. "Der Zornesbecher," *OTS* 15 (1969) 177-192.

1079 Barbour, R. S. "Gethsemane in the Tradition of the Passion," *NTS* 16 (1969-70) 231-251.

1080 van Unnik, W. C. " 'Alles ist dir möglich,' (Mk. 14,36)," *Verborum Veritas*. Ed. O. Böcher and K. Haacker (Fest. G. Stählin). Wuppertal: 1970, 27-36.

1081 Vanhoye, A. "L'agnoisse du Christ," *Christus* 18 (1971) 382-389.

1082 Kelber, W. H. "Mark 14,32-42: Gethsemane. Passion Christology and Discipleship Failure," *ZNW* 63 (1972) 166-187.

1083 Guillet, J. "Sorrowful unto Death," *Way* 13 (1973) 41-48.

1084 Mohn, W. "Gethsemane (Mk. 14,32-42)," *ZNW* 64 (1973) 194-208.

1085 Torris, J. "L'agonie Jésus (Marc 14,32-42). Intention, sources, historicité," *La Pensée et les hommes* 17 (1973) 75-77.

1086 Stein, R. H. "A Short Note on Mark XIV.28 and XVI. 7," *NTS* 20 (1974) 445-452.

1087 Feuillet, A. "Le récit lucanien de l'agonie de Gethsémani (Lc. xxii,39-46)," *NTS* 22 (1975-76) 399-417.

1088 Kelber, W. H. "The Hour of the Son of Man and the Temptation of the Disciples (Mark 14:32-42)," *The Passion in Mark: Studies on Mark 14-16*. Ed. W. H. Kelber. Philadelphia: 1976, 41-60.

1089 Schneider, G. "Engel und Blutschweiss. (Luk. 22,43-44)," *BZ* 20 (1976) 112-116.

1090 Szarek, G. "A Critique of Kelber's 'The Hour of the Son of Man and the Temptation of the Disciples: Mark 14:32-42'," SBLASP (1976), 111-118.

1091 Larkin, W. J. "The Old Testament Background of Luke xxii.43-44," *NTS* 25 (1978-79) 250-253.

1092 Blaising, C. A. "Gethsemane: A Prayer of Faith," *JETS* 22 (1979), 333-343.

1093 Léon-Dufour, X. "Jésus à Gethsémani. Essai de lecture synchronique," *ScEs* 31 (1979) 251-268.

1094 Neyrey, J. H. "The Absence of Jesus' Emotions—the Lucan Redaction of Lk. 22,39-46," *Bib* 61 (1980) 153-171.

1095 Tostengard, S. "Luke 22:39-46," *Int* 1980) 283-288.

1096 Duplacy, J. "La préhistorie du texte en Luc 22:43-44," *New Testament Textual Criticism. Its Significance for Exegesis*. Ed. E. J. Epp and G. D. Fee (Fest. B. M. Metzger). Oxford: 1981, 77-86.

1097 Thomas, J. "La scéne du jardin selon Marc 14,32-42," *Christus* 111 (1981) 350-360.

1098 Grassi, J. A. "Abba, Father (Mark 14,36): Another Approach," *JAAR* 50 (1982) 449-458.

1099 Phillips, G. A. "Gethsemane: Spirit and Discipleship in Mark's Gospel," *The Journey of Western Spirituality*. Ed. A. W. Sadler. Chico, CA: 1982, 49-63.

1100 Ehrman, B. D. and Plunkett, M. A. "The Angel and the Agony: The Textual Problem of Luke 22:43-44," *CBQ* 45 (1983) 401-416.

1101 Lods, M. "Climat de bataille à Gethsemane," *ETR* 60 (1985) 425-429.

1102 Soards, M. L. "Understanding Luke 22.39," *BT* 36 (1985) 336-337.

1103 Green, J. B. "Jesus on the Mount of Olives (Luke 22:39-46): Tradition and Theology," *JSNT* 26 (1986) 29-48.

1104 Kiley, M. " 'Lord, Save My Life' (Ps 116:4) as Generative Text for Jesus' Gethsemane Prayer (Mark 14:36a)," *CBQ* 48 (1986) 655-659.

1105 Söding, T. "Gebet und Gebetsmahnung Jesu in Getsemani. Eine redaktionskritische Auslegung von Mk 14,32-42," *BZ* 31 (1987) 76-100.

1106 Aagaard, A. M. "Doing God's Will. Matthew 26:36-46," *International Review of Mission* 77 (1988) 221-228.

1107 Baarda, T. "Luke 22:42-47a. The Emperor Julian as a Witness to the Text of Luke," *NovT* 30 (1988) 289-296.

1108 Beck, B. "Gethsemane in the Four Gospels," *Epworth Review* 15 (1988) 57-65.

1109 Martin, F. "Literary Theory, Philosophy of History and Exegesis," *Thomist* 52 (1988) 575-604.

XIII. The Betrayal and Arrest of Jesus; Judas the Betrayer

Books

1110 Haugg, D. *Judas Iskarioth in den neutestamentlichen Berichten.* Freiburg: 1930.

1111 Halas, R. B. *Judas Iscariot.* Washington: 1946.

1112 Buchheit, G. *Judas Iscarioth: Legende, Geschichte, Deutung.* Gütersloh: 1954.

1113 Lüthi, K. *Judas Iskarioth.* Zurich: 1955.

1114 Gärtner, B. *Iscariot.* Trans. V. I. Gruhn. Philadelphia: 1971.

1115 Goldschmidt, H. L. and Limbeck, M. *Heilvoller Verrat? Judas im Neuen Testament.* Stuttgart: 1976.

1116 Heuter, J. E. *Matthew, Mark, Luke, John...Now Judas and His Redemption (In Search of the Real Judas).* Brookline Village, MA.: 1983.

1117 Vogler, W. *Judas Iskarioth. Untersuchungen zu Tradition und Redaktion von Textes des Neuen Testaments und ausserkanonischer Schriften.* TA 42. Berlin: 1983.

1118 Wagner, H. (ed.). *Judas Iskariot. Menschliches oder heilsgeschichtliches Drama?* Frankfurt: 1985.

1119 Klauck, H. J. *Judas—ein Jünger des Herrn.* QD 111. Freiberg/Basel/Vienna: 1987.

1120 Schwarz, G. *Jesus und Judas. Aramäistische Untersuchungen zur Jesus-Judas Überlieferung der Evangelien und der Apostelgeschichte.* BWANT 123. Stuttgart/Berlin/ Cologne/Mainz: 1988.

Articles

1121 Chadwick, G. A. "Judas Iscariot," *Exp* 3rd ser. 10 (1889) 161-174.

1122 MacDonald, D. "Malchus' Ear," *ExpT* 10 (1898-99) 188.

1123 Wrede, W. "Judas Iscarioth in der Christlichen Überlieferung," *Vorträge und Studien.* Tübingen: 1907, 127-146.

1124 Cox, W. A. "Judas Iscariot," *Interpreter* 3 (1907) 414-422; 4 (1908) 218-219.

1125 Nestle, E. "Zum Judaskuss," *ZNW* 15 (1914) 92-93.

1126 Schläger, G. "Die Ungeschichtlichkeit des Verräters Judas," *ZNW* 15 (1914) 50-59.

1127 Plath, M. "Warum hat die urchristliche Gemeinde auf die Überlieferung der Judaserzählungen Wert gelegt?" *ZNW* 17 (1916) 178-188.

1128 Burn, J. H. "St. Mark xiv.10," *ExpT* 28 (1916-17) 278-279.

1129 Wright, A. "Was Judas Iscariot 'The First of the Twelve'?" *JTS* 18 (1916-17) 32-34.

1130 Bacon, B. W. "What did Judas Betray?" *HibJ* 19 (1920-21) 476-493.

1131 Hingston, J. H. "John 18,5-6," *ExpT* 32 (1920-21) 232.

1132 Deissmann, A. " 'Friend, wherefore art thou come?'," *ExpT* 33 (1921-22) 491-493.

1133 Owen, E. C. E. "St. Matthew xxvi.50," *JTS* 29 (1927-28) 384-386.

1134 Smisson, E. A. "Mark XIV.41: *apechei*," *ExpT* 40 (1928-29) 528.

1135 Spiegelberg, W. "Der Sinn von *eph' hō parei* in Mt. 26.50," *ZNW* 28 (1929) 341-343.

1136 Klostermann, E. "Zu Spiegelbergers Aufsatz 'Der Sinn von *eph' hō parei* in Mat. 26.50" *ZNW* 29 (1930) 311.

1137 Wilson, J. P. "Matthew xxvi.50: 'Friend, wherefore art thou come?'," *ExpT* 41 (1929-30) 334.

1138 Lendrum, J. "The Impression from the Gospels that All was fixed Beforehand," *ExpT* 42 (1930-31) 345-350.

1139 Joüon, P. "Luc XXII,50-51: *to ous tou ōtiou*," *RSR* 24 (1934) 473-474.

1140 Rostovtzeff, M. *"Ous dexion apotemnein,"* *ZNW* 33 (1934) 196-199.

1141 Huby, J. "Un double problème de critique textuelle et d'interpretation: Saint Jean xviii,11-12," *RSR* 27 (1937) 408-421.

1142 Emmet, P. B. "St. Mark xiv.45," *ExpT* 50 (1938-39) 93.

1143 Torrey, C. C. "The Name 'Iscariot'," *HTR* 36 (1943) 51-62.

1144 Nolle, L. "The Young Man in Mark XIV, 51," *Scr* 2 (1947) 113-114.

1145 Harrison, E. F. "Jesus and Judas," *BSac* 105 (1948) 170-181.

1146 Knox, J. "A note on Mark 14:51-52," *The Joy of Study*. Ed. S. E. Johnson (Fest. F. C. Grant). New York: 1951, 27-30.

1147 Argyle, A. W. "The Meaning of Mark xiv.49," *ExpT* 63 (1951-52), 354.

1148 Belcher, F. W. "A Comment on Mark xiv.45," *ExpT* 64 (1952-53) 240.

1149 Dibelius, M. "Jesus und der Judaskuss," *Botschaft und Geschichte*. Tübingen: 1953, I: 272-277.

1150 Mein, P. "A Note on John xviii.5, 6," *ExpT* 65 (1953-54) 286-287.

1151 Boobyer, G. H. *"APECHEI* in Mark xiv.41," *NTS* 2 (1955-56) 44-48.

1152 Lüthi, K. "Das Problem des Judas Iskarioth—neu untersucht," *EvT* 16 (1956) 98-114.

1153 Buchanan, G. W. "Mark xiv.43," *ExpT* 68 (1956-57) 27.

1154 Krieger, N. "Der Knecht des Hohenpriesters," *NovT* (1957) 73-74.

1155 Doeve, J. W. "Die Gefangennahme Jesu in Gethsemane," *SE* I (TU 73, 1959) 458-480.

1156 Daube, D. "Three Notes having to do with Johanan ben Zaccai," *JTS* 11 (1960) 59-61.

1157 Kosmala, H. "Matthew xxvi 52—A Quotation from the Targum," *NovT* 4 (1960) 3-5.

1158 Rehkopf, F. "Mt. 26,50: *hetaire, eph' hō parei*," *ZNW* 52 (1961) 109-115.

1159 Reynen, H. *"Synagesthai*, Joh. 18,2," *BZ* 5 (1961) 86-90.

1160 Schelkle, K. H. *"Synagesthai*, Joh. 18,2," *BZ* 5 (1961) 86-91.

1161 Cullmann, O. "Le douzième apôtre," *RHPR* 42 (1962) 133-140. = "Der Zwölfte Apostel," *Vorträge und Aufsätze*. Tübingen: 1966, 214-222.

1162 Eltester, W. " 'Freund, wozu du gekommen bist' (Mt. xxvi 50)," *Neotestamentica et Patristica* (Fest. O. Cullmann). *NovTSup* 6. Leiden: 1962, 70-91.

1163 Fischer, L. R. "Betrayed by Friends. An Expository Study of Ps. 22," *Int* 26 (1964) 20-27.

1164 Schwank, B. "Jesus überschreitet den Kidron (18,1-11)," *Sein und Sendung* 29 (1964) 3-15.

1165 Bishop, E. F. F. "Guide to those who Arrested Jesus," *EvQ* 40 (1968) 41-42.

1166 Lee, G. M. "Matthew xxvi.50 *Hetaire, eph hō parei*," *ExpT* 81 (1969-70) 55.

1167 Richter, G. "Die Gefangennahme Jesu nach dem Johannesevangelium (18,1-12)," *BibLeb* 10 (1969) 26-39.

1168 Vanhoye, A. "La fuite du jeune homme nu (Mc 14,51-52)," *Bib* 52 (1971) 401-406.

1169 Enslin, M. S. "How the Story Grew: Judas in Fact and Fiction," *Festschrift to Honor F. Wilbur Gingrich*. Ed. E. H. Barth and E. E. Cocroft. Leiden: 1972, 123-141.

1170 Schneider, G. "Die Verhaftung Jesu. Traditionsgeschichte von Mk. 14,43-52," *ZNW* 63 (1972), 188-209.

1171 Glasson, T. F. "Davidic Links with the Betrayal of Jesus," *ExpT* 85 (1974) 118-119.

1172 Trudinger, L. P. "Davidic Links in the Betrayal of Jesus: Some Further Observations," *ExpT* 86 (1975) 278-279.

1173 Lapide, P. E. "Verräter oder verraten? Judas in evangelischer und jüdischer Sicht," *Lutherische Monatshefte* 16 (1977) 75-79.

1174 Richter, G. "Die Gefangennahme Jesu nach dem Johannesevangelium," *Studien zum Johannesevangelium*. Regensburg 1977, 74-87.

1175 Sabbe, M. "The Arrest of Jesus in Jn. 18,1-11 and its Relation to the Synoptic Gospels," *L'Évangile de Jean. Sources, rédaction, théologie*. Ed. M. de Jonge. BETL 44. Gembloux: 1977, 203-234.

1176 Ehrman, A. "Judas Iscariot and Abba Saqqara," *JBL* 97 (1978) 572-573.

1177 Fledderman, H. "The Flight of a Naked Young Man (Mark 14:51 52)," *CBQ* 41 (1979) 412-418.

1178 Neirynck, F. "La fuite du jeune homme en Mc. 15,51-52," *ETL* 55 (1979) 43-66.

1179 Charbonneau, A. "L'arrestation de Jésus, une victoire d'après la facture interne de Jn. 18.1-11," *ScEs* 34 (1982) 155-170.

1180 Limbeck, M. " 'Stecke dein Schwert in die Scheide . . .!' Die Jesusbewegung im Unterschied zu den Zeloten," *BK* 37 (1982) 98-104.

1181 Schnellbächer, E. L. "Das Rätsel des *neaniskos* bei Markus," *ZNW* 73 (1982) 127-135.

1182 Roquefort, D. "Judas: Une figure de la perversion," *ETR* 58 (1983) 501-513.

1183 Cosby, M. R. "Mark 14:51-52 and the Problem of Gospel Narrative," *PRS* 11 (1984) 219-231.

1184 Crossan II, R. D. "Matthew 26:47-56—Jesus Arrested," *Tradition as Openness to the Future*. Ed. F. O. Francis (Fest. W. W. Fisher). Lanham: 1984, 175-190.

1185 Stein-Schneider, H. "A la recherche du Judas historique," *ETR* 60 (1985) 403-424.

1186 McVann, M. "Conjectures About a Guilty Bystander: The Sword Slashing in Mark 14:47," *Listening* 21 (1986) 124-137.

1187 Müller, K. W. "*APECHEI* (Mk 14:41)—absurda lectio?" *ZNW* 77 (1986) 83-100.

1188 Fortna, R. T. "Sayings of the Suffering and Risen Christ. The Quadruple Tradition," *Forum* 3 (1987) 63-69.

1189 Parrish, G. "In Defense of the Eleven," *Faith and Freedom* 40 (1987) 91-94.

1190 Peri, I. "Der Weggefährte," *ZNW* 78 (1987) 127-131.

1191 Suggit, J. "Comrade Judas: Matthew 26:50," *JTSAfrica* 63 (1988) 56-58.

See also 0127, 0254, 0409, 0431, 0434, 0444, 0454, 0460, 0550, 0774, 0836, 0884, 1250, 1467, 1638

XIV. The Trial
before the Sanhedrin

Books

1192 Innes, A. T. *The Trial of Jesus*. Edinburgh: 1899.

1193 Philippson, L. *Haben die Juden wirklich Jesus gekreuzigt? 2d. ed. Berlin: 1901.*

1194 Bevan, E. R. *Jerusalem under the High Priests*. London: 1904.

1195 Chauvin, C. *Le procès de Jésus-Christ*. Paris: 1904.

1196 Rosadi, G. *The Trial of Jesus*. New York: 1905.

1197 Buss, S. *Trial of Jesus. Illustrated from Talmud and Roman Law*. London: 1906.

1198 Drucker, A. P. *The Trial of Jesus from Jewish Sources*. New York: 1907.

1199 Chandler, W. M. *The Trial of Jesus from a Lawyer's Standpoint*. 2 vols. New York: 1908.

1200 Stalker, J. *Das Verhör und der Tod Jesu*. Leipzig: 1908.

1201 Juster, J. *Les Juifs dans l'Empire Romain*. 2 vols. Paris: 1914.

1202 Husband, R. W. *The Prosecution of Jesus*. Princeton: 1916.

1203 Doerr , F. *Der Prozess Jesu in rechtsgeschichtlicher Beleuchtung*. Berlin: 1920.

1204 Biser, A. C. *The Trial of Jesus Christ*. Chicago: 1925.

1205 Campbell, W. A. *Did the Jews Kill Jesus? New York: 1927.*

1206 Aicher, G. *Der Prozess Jesu*. Bonn: 1929.

1207 Radin, M. *The Trial of Jesus of Nazareth*. Chicago: 1931.

1208 Goldin, H. E. *The Case of the Nazarene Reopened*. New York: 1948.

1209 Powell, F. J. *The Trial of Jesus Christ*. London: 1949.

1210 Bammel, E. *Kaiphas und der Prozess Jesu*. Coburg: 1951.

1211 Hoenig, S. B. *The Great Sanhedrin*. Philadelphia: 1953.

1212 Kilpatrick, G. D. *The Trial of Jesus*. London: 1953.

1213 Brandon, S. G. F. *The Fall of Jerusalem and the Christian Church: A Study of the Effects of the Jewish Overthrow of A.D. 70 on Christianity*. 2d ed. London: 1957, repr. 1968.

1214 Carmichael, J. *The Death of Jesus*. 2d ed. London: 1963.

1215 Mantel, H. *Studies in the History of the Sanhedrin*. Cambridge: 1965.

1216 Achter, V. *Der Prozess gegen Jesus von Nazareth*. Cologne: 1964.

1217 MacRuer, J. C. *The Trial of Jesus*. Toronto: 1964.

1218 Koch, W. *Der Prozess Jesu. Versuch eines Tatsachenberichts*. Cologne: 1966.

1219 Isorin, J. *Le vrai procès de Jésus*. Paris: 1967.

1220 Koch, W. *Zum Prozess Jesu. Mit Beiträgen von J. Blinzler, G. Klein, P. Winter*. Weiden: 1967.

1221 Brandon, S. G. F. *The Trial of Jesus of Nazareth*. London: 1968.

1222 Blinzler, J. *Der Prozess Jesus*, 4 ed. Regensburg: 1969. Eng. Trans. of 2 ed: *The Trial of Jesus*. Trans. J. and F. McHugh. Westminster, MD: 1959.

1223 Bammel, E. ed. *The Trial of Jesus: Cambridge Studies in honour of C. F. D. Moule*. SBT 2d Ser 13. Naperville, IL.: 1970.

1224 Cohn, H. *The Trial and Death of Jesus*. New York: 1970.

1225 Wilson, W. R. *The Execution of Jesus: A Judicial, Literary and Historical Investigation*. New York: 1970.

1226 Catchpole, D. R. *The Trial of Jesus: A Study in the Gospels and Jewish Historiography from 1770 to the Present Day*. SPB 18. Leiden: 1972.

1227 Gorman, R. *The Trial of Christ: A Reappraisal*. Huntington: 1972.

1228 Sloyan, G. S. *Jesus on Trial: The Development of the Passion Narratives and their Historical and Ecumenical Implications*. Philadelphia: 1973.

1229 Winter, P. *On the Trial of Jesus*. 2d ed. Rev. and ed. T. A. Burkill and G. Vermes. Berlin: 1974.

1230 Strobel, A. *Die Stunde der Wahrheit. Untersuchungen zum Strafverfahren gegen Jesus*. WUNT 21. Tübingen: 1980.

1231 Imbert, J. *Le procès de Jésus, "Que sais-je?"*. Paris: 1980.

1232 Rivkin, E. *What Crucified Jesus: The Political Execution of a Charismatic*. Nashville: 1984.

1233 Fricke, W. *Standrechtlich gekreuzigt. Person und Prozess des Jesus aus Galiläa*. Frankfurt am Main: 1986.

1234 Lapide, P. E. *Wer war schuld an Jesu Tod?* Gütersloh: 1987.

1235 Kertelge, K. (ed.) *Der Prozess gegen Jesus. Historische Ruckfrage und theologische Deutung*. QD 112. Freiburg/ Basel/ Vienna: 1988.

1236 Pesch, R. *Der Prozess Jesu geht weiter*. Freiburg/ Basel/ Vienna: 1988.

Articles

1237 Langen, J. "Das jüdische Synedrium und die römische Prokuratur in Judäa," *TQ* 44 (1862) 411-463.

1238 Schürer, E. "Die *archiereus* im Neuen Testament," *Theologische Studien und Kritiken* 45 (1872) 593-657.

1239 Gardiner, F. "On the Aorist *apesteilen* in Jn. xviii.24," *JBL* 6 (1886) 45-55

1240 Farquhar, J. M. "The First Trial of Christ," *ExpT* 6 (1894-95) 284-288, 429-431.

1241 Findlay, G. G. "The Connexion of John xviii.12-28," *ExpT* 6 (1894-95) 335-336, 478-79.

1242 Wright, A. "The First Trial of Jesus," *ExpT* 6 (1894-95) 523-524.

1243 Innes, A. T. "The Trials of Jesus Christ," *ExpT* 10 (1898-99) 522-523.

1244 Lamb, F. J. "The Trial of Jesus: Its Value in the Foundation of the Faith," *BibSac* 56 (1899) 223-240.

1245 MacGregor, W. M. "Christ's Three Judges," *Exp* 6th ser. 2 (1900) 59-68, 119-129.

1246 Kreyenbuhl, J. "Der Ort der Verurteilung Jesu," *ZNW* 3 (1902) 15-22.

1247 Cheever, H. M. "The Legal Aspects of the Trial of Christ," *BibSac* 60 (1903) 495-509.

1248 Burkitt, F. C. "On Romans IX, 5 and Mark XIV, 61," *JTS* 5 (1904) 453-454.

1249 Goguel, M. "Juifs et Romains dans l'historie de la Passion," *RHR* 72 (1910) 165-182; 295-322.

1250 Price, O. J. "Jesus' Arrest and Trial," *Biblical World* 36 (1910) 345-353.

1251 Kastner, K. "Nochmals die Verspottung Christ," *BZ* 9 (1911) 56.

1252 Klövekorn, P. B. "Jesus vor der jüdischen Behörde," *BZ* 9 (1911) 266-276.

1253 Boswell, R. B. "Destroying and Rebuilding the Temple," *ExpT* 26 (1914-15) 140-141.

1254 Easton, B. S. "The Trial of Jesus," *AJT* 19 (1915) 430-452.

1255 White, W. G. "Mark, xiv.55, 56," *ExpT* 23 (1917-18) 138-139.

1256 Danby, H. "The Bearing of the Rabbinical Criminal Code on the Jewish Trial Narratives in the Gospels," *JTS* 21 (1920) 54-55.

1257 Barton, G. A. "On the Trial of Jesus before the Sanhedrin," *JBL* 42 (1922) 205-211.

1258 Abrahams, I. "The Tannaite Tradition and the Trial Narratives," *Studies in Pharisaism and the Gospels*. Cambridge: 1924, 129-137.

1259 Rudberg, G. "Die Verhöhnung Jesu vor dem Hohenpriester," *ZNW* 24 (1925) 307-309.

1260 Harris, J. R. "A Lost Verse in the Gospel of Mark," *ExpT* 39 (1927-28) 456-458.

1261 Cooke, H. P. "Christ Crucified—and by Whom" *HeyJ* 30 (1930) 61-74.

1262 van Unnik, W. C. "Jesu Verhöhnung vor dem Synedrium (Mc 14,65 par)," *ZNW* 29 (1930) 310-311.

1263 Büchsel, F. "Die Blutgerichtsbarkeit des Synedrions," *ZNW* 30 (1931) 202-210.

1264 Lietzmann, H. "Der Prozess Jesu," *Sitzungsberichte der Preussischen Akademie der Wissenschafter, phil.— hist. Klasse*. Berlin: 1931, 313-322. = *Kleine Schriften*. Berlin: 1958, 2:251-263.

1265 Lietzmann, H. "Bemerkungen zum Prozess Jesu I. II.," *ZNW* 30 (1931), 211-215; 31 (1932), 78-84 = *Kleine Schriften*. Berlin: 1958, 2:264-268, 269-276.

1266 Fiebig, P. "Der Prozess Jesu," *TSK* 104 (1932) 213-218.

1267 Goguel, M. "À propos du procès de Jesu," *ZNW* 31 (1932) 289-301.

1268 Kosmala, H. "Der Prozess Jesu," *Saat auf Hoffnung* 69 (1932) 25-39.

1269 Vincent, L. H. "L'Antonia et le Prétoire," *RB* 42 (1933) 83-113.

1270 Büchsel, F. "Noch einmal: Zur Blutgerichtsbarkeit des Synedrions," *ZNW* 33 (1934) 84-87.

1271 Bickerman, E. "Utilitas crucis. Observations sur les récits du procès de Jésus dans les Évangiles canoniques," *RSR* 112 (1935) 169-241.

1272 Lengel, J. "Zum Prozess Jesu," *Hermes* 70 (1935) 312-321.

1273 Robinson, W. C. "The Greater Confession," *EvQ* 7 (1935) 364-377.

1274 Ebeling, H. J. "Zur Frage nach der Kompetenz des Synedrions," *ZNW* 35 (1936) 290-295.

1275 Holzmeister, U. "Zur Frage der Blutgerichtsbarkeit des Synedriums," *Bib* 19 (1938) 43-59; 151-174.

1276 Benoit, P. "Le procès de Jésus," *Vie Intellectuelle* 25 (1940) 200-213; 372-378, 54-64 *Exégèse et théologie*. Paris: 1961, 1:265-289 = *Exegese und Theologie*. Düsseldorf: 1965, 1:113-132. Eng. trans.: "The Trial of Jesus," *Jesus and Gospel*. Trans. B. Weatherhead. New York: 1973, 123-146.

1277 Zeitlin, S. "The Crucifixion of Jesus Re-examined," *JQR* 31 (1941) 327-369; 32 (1942) 175-189; 279-301.

1278 Benoit, P. "Jésus devant le sanhedrin," *Aug* 20 (1943) 143-165. = *Exégèse et théologie*. Paris: 1961, 1:265-289 = *Exegese und Theologie*. Düsseldorf: 1965, 1:133-148. Eng. trans: "Jesus Before the Sanhedrin," *Jesus and Gospel*. Trans. B. Weatherhead. New York: 1973, 147-166.

1279 Schmidt, K. L. "The Todesprozess Jesu," *Jud* 1 (1945), 1-40.

1280 Kleist, J. A. "The Two False Witnesses (Mk. 14,55 ff.)," *CBQ* 9 (1947) 321-323.

1281 Leroux, M. "Responsabilités dans le procès du Christ," *CahS* 1 (1947) 102-121.

1282 Ernest, K. J. "Did the Jews Kill Jesus? A Reply," *Int* 1 (1947) 376-378.

1283 Gaechter, P. "The Hatred of the House of Annas," *TS* 8 (1947) 3-37.

1284 Sizoo, J. R. "Did the Jews Kill Jesus? Historical Criticism in the Pulpit," *Int* 1 (1947) 201-206.

1285 Goguel, M. "Le procès de Jésus," *FV* 47 (1949) 395-403.

1286 Besnier, R. "Le procès du Christ," *RHR* 18 (1950) 191-209.

1287 Jeremias, J. "Zur Geschichtlichkeit des Verhörs Jesu vor dem Hohen Rat," *ZNW* 43 (1950-51) 145-150.

1288 Meinertz, M. "Der Prozess Jesu," *HLVG* 83 (1951) 7-13.

1289 Cantinat, J. "Jésus devant le Sanhedrin," *NRT* 75 (1953) 300-308.

1290 Bammel, E. "Die Bruderfolge im Hochpriestertum der herodianisch—römanischen Zeit," *ZDPV* 70 (1954), 147-153.

1291 Vincent, L. H. "L'Antonia, palais primitive d'Herode," *RB* 61 (1954) 87-107.

1292 Elias, J. "Erwählung als Gabe und Aufgabe. Eine Analyse des Jesu-Prozesses," *Jud* 2 (1955) 29-49; 89-108.

1293 Robinson, J. A. T. "The Second Coming. Mark 14,62," *ExpT* 67 (1955-56) 336-340.

1294 Winter, P. "Luke XXII.66b-71," *ST* 9 (1955-56) 112-115.

1295 Buchanan, G. W. "Mark XIV.54," *ExpT* 68 (1956) 27.

1296 Burkill, T. A. "The Competence of the Sanhedrin," *VC* 10 (1956) 1-18.

1297 Rosenblatt, J. "The Crucifixion of Jesus from the Standpoint of Pharisaic Law," *JBL* 75 (1956) 314-321.

1298 Schneider, J. "Zur Komposition von Joh. xviii,12-27 Kaiaphas und Hannas," *ZNW* 48 (1957) 111-119.

1299 Stonehouse, N. B. "Who Crucified Jesus?" *Paul before the Areopagus and other NT Studies.* London: 1957.

1300 Ostrow, J. "Tannaitic and Roman Procedure in Homicide," *JQR* 48 (1957-58) 352-370; 52 (1961-62) 160-167; 245-263.

1301 Burkill, T. A. "The Trial of Jesus," *VC* 12 (1958) 1-20.

1302 Beilner, W. "Prozess und Verurteilung Jesu," *Christus und die Pharisäer.* Vienna: 1959, 235-239.

1303 Flusser, D. "Two Notes on the Midrash on 2 Sam. VII," *IEJ* (1959) 99-109.

1304 Klijn, A. F. J. "Scribes, Pharisees, Highpriests and Elders in the NT," *NovT* (1959) 259-267.

1305 Tyson, J. B. "The Lukan Version of the Trial of Jesus," *NovT* 3 (1959) 249-258.

1306 Winter, P. "Marginal Notes on the Trial of Jesus," *ZNW* 50 (1959) 14-33; 221-251.

1307 Gundry, R. "*LMTLYM*. 1Q Isaiah a 50,6 and Mark 14,65," *RevQ* 2 (1960) 559-567.

1308 Blinzler, J. "Das Synedrium von Jerusalem und die Strassprozessordnung der Mischna," *ZNW* 52 (1961) 54-65.

1309 Braumann, G. "Markus 15,2-5 und Markus 14,55-64," *ZNW* 52 (1961) 273-278.

1310 Lohse, E. "Der Prozess Jesu Christi," *Ecclesia und Res Publica* (Fest. K. D. Schmidt). Göttingen: 1961, 24-39. = *Die Einheit des Neuen Testaments*. Göttingen: 1973, 88-103.

1311 Maier, J. "Ein neues Buch über den Prozess Jesu," *Jud* 17 (1961) 249-253.

1312 Verdam, P. J. "Sanhedrin en Gebbatha: A Few Necessary Additions to the Literature on the Trial of Jesus," *Free University Quarterly* 7 (1961) 259-287.

1313 Benoit, P. "Les outrages à Jésus Prophète (Mc XIV,65 par)," *Neotestamentica et Patristica* (Fest. O. Cullmann). Leiden: 1962, 92-110. = *Exégèse et Théologie*. Paris: 1965, 3:251-269.

1314 de la Potterie, I. "Deux livres récents sur le procès de Jésus," *Bib* 43 (1962) 87-93.

1315 Dodd, C. H. "The Prophecy of Caiaphas," *Neotestamentica et Patristica*. (Fest O. Cullmann). NovTSup 6. Leiden: 1962, 134-143.

1316 Kennard, J. S. Jr. "The Provincial Assembly," *ZNW* 53 (1962) 25-51.

1317 Lamarche, P. "Le 'blasphème' de Jésus devant le sanhedrin," *RSR* 50 (1962) 74-85.

1318 Nineham, D. "Review of J. Blinzler, *The Trial of Jesus* (1959), and of P. Winter, *On the Trial of Jesus* (1961)," *JTS* 19 (1962) 387-391.

1319 Schubert, K. "Die Juden oder die Römer?" *Wort und Wahrheit* 17 (1962) 701-710.

1320 Smallwood, E. M. "High Priests and Politics in Roman Palestine," *JTS* 13 (1962) 14-34.

1321 Winter, P. "Markus 14,53b. 55-64 ein Gebilde des Evangelisten," *ZNW* 53 (1962) 260-263.

1322 Schubert, K. "Die Juden und die Römer. Betrachtungen zur Geschichtlichkeit des Evangelienberichts vom Prozess vor dem Hohenpriester," *BibLeb* (1962-63) 235-242.

1323 Duplacy, J. "Une variante méconnue du texte recu: *ē apolysēte* (Lc 22,68)," *Neutestamentliche Aufsätze*. Ed. J. Blinzler, O. Kuss, and F. Mussner (Fest. J. Schmid). Regensburg: 1963, 42-52.

1324 Lindeskog, G. "Der Prozess Jesu im jüdisch-christlichen Religionsgespräch," *Abraham, unser Vater*. Ed. O. Betz, M. Hengel and P. Schmidt (Fest. O. Michel). Leiden: 1963, 325-336.

1325 Schalit, A. "Kritische Randbemerkungen zu Paul Winter's *On the Trial of Jesus*," *ASTI* 2 (1963) 86-102.

1326 Schweizer, E. "Der Prozess Jesu," *Kirchenblatt für die reformierte Schweiz* 119 (1963) 146-150.

1327 Winter, P. "The Marcan Account of Jesus' Trial by the Sanhedrin," *JTS* 14 (1963) 94-102.

1328 Winter, P. "The Trial of Jesus and the Competence of the Sanhedrin," *NTS* 10 (1963-64) 494-499.

1329 Jaubert, A. "Les séances du Sanhédrin et des récits de la passion," *RHR* 166 (1964), 143-169.

1330 Reichrath, H. "Der Prozess Jesu," *Jud* 20 (1964) 129-155.

1331 Tcherikover, V. A. "Was Jerusalem a Polis?" *IEJ* 14 (1964) 61-78.

1332 Bartsch, H. W. "Wer verurteilte Jesus zum Tode? Zu den Rezensionen des Buches von Paul Winter: *On the Trial of Jesus*," *NovT* (1964-65) 210-217.

1333 Zeitlin, S. "The Crucifixion, a Libelous Accusation against the Jews," *JQR* 55 (1964-65) 8-22.

1334 Catchpole, D. R. "You have heard His Blasphemy," *The Tyndale House Bulletin* 16 (1965) 10-18.

1335 Jaubert, A. "Les séances du Sanhédrin et les récits de la passion (suite), " *RHR* 167 (1965) 1-33.

1336 Mahoney, A. "A New Look at an Old Problem (John 18:12-14, 19-24)," *CBQ* 27 (1965) 137-144.

1337 Schumann, H. "Bemerkungen zum Prozess Jesu vor dem Synhedrium" *ZRGG* 82 (1965) 315-320.

1338 Winter, P. "The Trial of Jesus," *Commentary* 38 (1964) 35-41; 39 (1965) 10-28.

1339 Brandon, S. G. F. "The Trial of Jesus," *History Today* 16 (1966) 251-259.

1340 Trilling, W. "Der Prozess Jesu," *Fragen zur Geschichtlichkeit Jesu*. Düsseldorf: 1966, 130-141.

1341 Cohn, H. "Reflections on the Trial and Death of Jesus," *Israel Law Review* 2 (1967) 332-379.

1342 Schubert, K. "Das Verhör Jesu vor dem Hohen Rat," *Bibel und Zeitgemässer Glaube*. Ed. J. Sint. Klosterneuburg: 1967, 2:97-130.

1343 Winter, P. "Zum Prozess Jesu," *Antijudäismus im Neuen Testament?* Ed. W. P. Eckert, N. P. Levinson and M. Stohr. Munich: 1967, 95-104.

1344 Dabrowski, E. "The Trial of Jesus in Recent Research," *SE* IV (TU 102 1968) 21-27.

1345 Haufe, G. "Der Prozess Jesu im Lichte der gegenwärtigen Forschung," *ZdZ 22 (1968) 93-101.*

1346 Meyer, F. E. "Einige Bermerkungen zur Bedeutung des Terminus 'Synhedrion' in den Schriften des Neuen Testaments," *NTS* 14 (1968) 545-551.

1347 O'Neill, J. C. "The Silence of Jesus," *NTS* 15 (1968-69) 153-167.

1348 Bammel, E. "Ex illa itaque die consilium fecerunt . . .," *The Trial of Jesus.* Ed. E. Bammel, SBT 2d. ser. 13. Naperville, IL.: 1970, 11-40.

1349 Catchpole, D. R. "The Problem of the Historicity of the Sanhedrin Trial," *The Trial of Jesus.* Ed. E. Bammel. SBT 2d. ser. 13. Naperville, IL.: 1970, 47-65.

1350 Derrett, J. D. M. "An Oriental Lawyer Looks at the Trial of Jesus and the Doctrine of the Redemption," *Law in the New Testament.* London: 1970, 389-460.

1351 Enslin, M. S. "The Trial of Jesus," *JQR* 60 (1970) 353-355.

1352 Gnilka, J. "Die Verhandlungen vor dem Synhedrium und vor Pilatus nach Markus 14:53-15:5," *EKKNT—* Vorarbeiten Heft 2. Zurich: 1970, 5-21.

1353 Kamelsky, J. "Über den Prozess und die Lehre Jesu," *Internationale Dialog Zeitschrift* 3 (1970) 149-162.

1354 Morgan, R. " 'Nothing more negative . . .' A Concluding Unscientific Postscript to the Historical Research on the Trial of Jesus," *The Trial of Jesus.* Ed. E. Bammel, SBT 2d. ser. 13. Naperville, IL.: 1970, 135-146.

1355 Schneider, G. "Gab es eine vorsynoptische Szene Jesus vor dem Synhedrium?" *NovT* 12 (1970) 22-39.

1356 Schneider, G. "Jesus vor dem Synedrium," *BibLeb* 11 (1970) 1-15.

1357 Aron, R. "Quelques réflexions sur le procès de Jésus," *Lumière et Vie* 20 (1971) 5-17.

1358 Blinzler, J. "The Trial of Jesus in the Light of History," *Judaism* 20 (1971) 49-55.

1359 Brandon, S. G. F. "The Trial of Jesus," *Judaism* 20 (1971) 43-48.

1360 Cohn, H. "Reflections on the Trial of Jesus," *Judaism* 20 (1971) 10-23.

1361 Flusser, D. "A Literary Approach to the Trial of Jesus," *Judaism* 20 (1971) 32-36.

1362 Grant, R. M. "The Trial of Jesus in the Light of History," *Judaism* 20 (1971) 37-42.

1363 Miller, D. L. "*EMPAIZEIN: Playing the Mock Game (Luke 22:63-64),*" *JBL* 90 (1971) 309-313.

1364 Norr, D. "Problems of Legal History in the Gospels," *Jesus in His Time*. Ed. H. J. Schultz. Trans. B. Watchorn. Philadelphia: 1971, 115-123.

1365 Sandmel, S. "The Trial of Jesus: Reservations," *Judaism* 20 (1971) 69-74.

1366 Valentin, P. "Les comparutions de Jésus devant le Sanhédrin," *RSR* 59 (1971) 230-236.

1367 Chevallier, M. A. "La comparution de Jésus devant Hanne et Caiphe (Jean 18,12-14 et 19-24)," *Neues Testament und Geschichte*. Ed. H. Baltensweiler and B. Reicke (Fest. O. Cullmann). Tübingen: 1972, 179-188.

1368 Feuter, K., Schweizer, E. and Winter, P. "Diskussion um den Prozess Jesu," *Wer war Jesus von Nazareth? Die Erforschung einer historischen Gestalt*. Ed. G. Strube. Munich: 1972, 221-240.

1369 Kremer, J. "Verurteilt als 'König der Juden' verkündigt als 'Herr und Christus'," *BLit* 45 (1972) 23-32.

1370 O'Meara, T. F. "The Trial of Jesus in an Age of Trials," *TToday* 28 (1972) 451-465.

1371 Schubert, K. "Kritik der Bibekritik. Dargestellt an Hand des Markusberichtes vom Verhör Jesus vor dem Synedrion," *WuW* 27 (1972) 421-434.

1372 Wallace, J. E. "The Trial of Jesus in an Age of Trials: A Legal Response," *TToday* 28 (1972) 466-469.

1373 Bowker, J. "The Offence and Trial of Jesus," *Jesus and the Pharisees*. Cambridge: 1973 42-52.

1374 Flusser, D. "Wer löste die Kreuzigung aus? Der 'Prozess Jesu' aus der Sicht jüdischer Forscher," *Lutherische Monatshefte* 12 (1973) 306-308.

1375 Bammel, E. "Die Blutgerichtsbarkeit in der römischen Provinz Judäa vor dem ersten jüdischen Aufstand," *JJS* 25 (1974) 35-49.

1376 Berger, K. "Die königlichen Messiastraditionen des Neuen Testaments," *NTS* 20 (1973-74) 1-44.

1377 Legasse, S. "Jésus devant le Sanhédrin. Recherche sur les traditions évangélique," *RTL* 5 (1974) 170-197.

1378 Maier, P. L. "Who was Responsible for the Trial and Death of Jesus? *Christianity Today* 18 (1974) 806-809.

1379 Müller, K. "Jesus und die Sadduzäer," *Biblische Randbemerkungen. Schülerfestschrift R. Schnackenburg*. Ed. H. Merklein and J. Lange. Würzburg: 1974, 3-24.

1380 Safrai, S. "VII. Jewish Self-Government," *The Jewish People in the First Century*. Ed. S. Safrai and M. Stern. Philadelphia: 1974, 1:379-400.

1381 de Jonge, M. "The Use of *HO CHRISTOS* in the Passion Narratives," *Jésus aux origines de la christologie. BETL* 40. Gembloux: 1975, 169-192.

1382 Rivkin, E. "Beth Din, Boulē, Sanhedrin: Tragedy of Errors," *HUCA* 46 (1975) 181-199.

1383 Stewart, R. A. "Judicial Procedure in New Testament Times," *EvQ* 47 (1975) 94-109.

1384 Walaskay, P. W. "The Trial and Death of Jesus in the Gospel of Luke," *JBL* 94 (1975) 81-93.

1385 Baumgarten, J. A. "The Duodecimal Courts of Qumran, Revelation and the Sanhedrin," *JBL* 95 (1976) 59-78.

1386 Donahue, J. R. "Temple, Trial, and Royal Christology (Mark 14:53-65)," *The Passion in Mark: Studies on Mark 14-16*. Ed. W. H. Kelber. Philadelphia: 1976, 61-79.

1387 Dormeyer, D. "The Passion Jesu als Ergebnis seines Konflikts mit führenden Kreisen des Judentums," *Gottesverächter und Menschenfeinde? Juden zwischen Jesus und frühchristlicher Kirche*. Ed. H. Goldstein. Düsseldorf: 1979, 211-228.

1388 Lapide, P. E. "Jesu Tode durch Römerhand. Zur blasphemischen These von 'Gottesmord' durch die Juden," *Gottesverächter und Menschenfeinde? Juden zwischen Jesus und frühchristlicher Kirche*. Ed. H. Goldstein. Düsseldorf: 1979, 239-255.

1389 Mussner, F. *Traktat über die Juden*. Munich: 1979, 293-305.

1390 Sloyan, G. S. "Recent Literature on the Trial Narratives of the Four Gospels," *Critical History and Biblical Faith: New Testament Perspectives*. Ed. T. J. Ryan. Villanora: 1979, 136-176.

1391 France, R. T. "Jésus devant Caïphe," *Hokhma* 15 (1980) 20-35.

1392 Anon. "Analyse de la véridiction. Procès de Jésus devant le Sanhedrin (Marc 14,55-65)," *SemiotBib* 27 (1982) 1-11.

1393 Betz, O. "Probleme des Prozesses Jesu," *Aufstieg und Niedergang der römischen Welt.* 25.1. Berlin: 1982, 565-647.

1394 Kempthorne, R. "Anti-Christian Tendency in pre-Marcan Traditions of the Sanhedrin Trial," *SE* VII (TU 126 1982) 283-286.

1395 Schinzer, R. "Die Bedeutung des Prozesses Jesu," *Neue Zeitschrift für systematische Theologie und Religionsphilosophie* 253 (1983) 138-154.

1396 Grundmann, W. "The decision of the Supreme Court to put Jesus to death (John 11:47-57) in its context: tradition and redaction in the Gospel of John," *Jesus and the Politics of His Day.* Ed. E. Bammel and C. F. D. Moule. Cambridge: 1984, 295-318.

1397 Pace, S. "The Statigraphy of the Text of Daniel and the Question of the Theological *Tendenz* in the Old Greek," *Bulletin of the International Organization for Septuagint and Cognate Studies* 17 (1984) 15-35.

1398 Schubert, K. "Biblical Criticism Criticised: with reference to the Markan report of Jesus' examination before the Sanhedrin," *Jesus and the Politics of His Day.* Ed. E. Bammel and C. F. D. Moule. Cambridge: 1984, 385-402.

1399 Ben-Chorin, S. "Wer hat Jesus zum Tode verurteilt?" *ZRGG* 37 (1985) 63-67.

1400 Hill, D. "Jesus Before the Sanhedrin—On What Charge?" *IBS* 7 (1985) 174-186.

1401 Black, M. "The Theological Appropriation of the Old Testament by the New Testament," *SJT* 39 (1986) 1-17.

1402 Flusser, D. "Who Is It that Struck You?" *Immanuel* 20 (1986) 27-32.

1403 Pawlikowski, J. T. "The Trial and Death of Jesus: Reflections in Light of a New Understanding of Judaism," *Chicago Studies* 25 (1986) 79-94.

1404 Beavis, M. A. "The Trial Before the Sanhedrin (Mark 14:53-65): A Reader's Response and Greco Roman Readers," *CBQ* 49 (1987) 581-596.

1405 Kolping, A. "Standrechtlich gekreuzigt." Neuere Überlegungen zum Prozess Jesu," *TRev* 83 (1987) 265-276.

1406 Ritt, H. "Wer war schuld am Jesu Tod? Zeitgeschichte, Recht und theologische Deutung," *BZ* 31 (1987) 167-175.

1407 Söding, T. "Der Prozess Jesu. Exegetische, historische und theologische Fragestellungen," *Herder Korrespondenz* 41 (1987) 236-240.

1408 Betz, O. "The Temple Scroll and the Trial of Jesus," *SWJT* 30 (1988) 5-8.

1409 Heil, J. P "Reader-Response and the Irony of Jesus before the Sanhedrin in Luke 22:66-71," *CBQ* 51 (1989) 271-284.

1410 Matera, F. J. "Luke 22,66-71: Jesus Before the *PRESBYTĒRION*," *ETL* 65 (1989) 43-59.

See also 0026, 0172, 0271, 0272, 0278, 0279, 0313, 0316, 0318, 0336, 0346, 0413, 0454, 0550, 1564, 1655, 1724

XV. Jesus' Answer
to the High Priest

Book

1411 Hay, D. M. *Glory at the Right Hand. Psalm 110 in Early Christianity*, SBLMS 18. Missoula: 1973.

Articles

1412 Tinsley, E. J. "The Sign of the Son of Man (Mk. 14,62)," *SJT* 8 (1955) 297-306.

1413 McArthur, H. K. "Mark xiv.62," *NTS* 4 (1957-58) 156-158.

1414 Scott, R. B. Y. "Behold, He Cometh with Clouds," *NTS* 5 (1958-59) 127-132.

1415 Glasson, T. F. "The Reply to Caiaphas (Mark XIV.62)," *NTS* 7 (4500-61) 88-93.

1416 Linton, P. "The Trial of Jesus and the Interpretation of Psalm CX," *NTS* 7 (1960-61) 258-262.

1417 Lövestam, E. "Die Frage des Hohenpriesters (Mark 14,61, par. Matth. 26,63)," *SEA* 26 (1961) 93-107.

1418 Mussner, F. "Die Wiederkunft des Menschensohnes nach Mk. 13,24-27 und 14,61-62," *BK* 16 (1961) 105-107.

1419 Feuillet, A. "Le triomphe du Fils de l'homme d'après la déclaration du Christ aux Sanhédrites (Mc., XIV,62; Mt., XXVI,64; Lc., XXII,69)," *La Venue du Messie*. Bruges: 1962, 149-171.

1420 Bartsch, H. W. "Tempelwort: ursprünglich entscheidener Anklagepunkt," *TZ* 20 (1964) 99-100.

1421 Goldberg, A. "Sitzend zur Rechten der Kraft," *BZ* 8 (1964) 284-293.

1422 Perrin, N. "Mark XIV 62: The End Product of a Christian Pesher Tradition?" *NTS* 12 (1965-66) 150-155.

1423 Borsch, F. H. "Mark XIV.62 and 1 Enoch LXII.5," *NTS* 14 (1967-68) 565-567.

1424 Ford, J. M. " 'The Son of Man'—An Euphemism," *JBL* 87 (1968) 257-266.

1425 O'Neill, J. C. "The Charge of Blaspehmy at Jesus' Trial before the Sanhedrin," *The Trial of Jesus.* Ed. E. Bammel, SBT 2d. ser. 13. Naperville, IL.: 1970, 72-77.

1426 Catchpole, D. R. "The Answer of Jesus to Caiaphas (Matt. xxvi.64)," *NTS* 17 (1971) 213-226.

1427 Seitz, O. F. J. "The Future Coming of the Son of Man: Three Midrashic Formulations in the Gospel of Mark," *SE* 6 (TU 112 1973) 478-494.

1428 Dupont, J. " 'Assis à la droite de Dieu.' L'interpretation du Ps. 110,1 dans le Nouveau Testament," *Resurrexit. Acts du Symposion sur la résurrection de Jésus.* Ed. E. Dhanis. Rome: 1974, 423-436.

1429 Perrin, N. "The High Priest's Question and Jesus' Answer, *The Passion in Mark: Studies on Mark 14-16."* Ed. W. H. Kelber. Philadelphia: 1976, 80-95.

1430 Kempthorne, R. "The Marcan Text of Jesus' Answer to the High Priest (Mark xiv 62)," *NovT* 19 (1977) 197-208.

1431 Derrett, J. D. M. "Midrash in the New Testament: the Origin of Luke xxii,67-68," *Studies in the New Testament.* Leiden: 1978, 2:184-193.

1432 Beasley-Murray, G. R. "Jesus and Apocalyptic: With Special Reference to Mark 14,62," *L'Apocalypse johannique et l'Apocalyptique dans le Nouveau Testament.* Ed. J. Lambrecht. BETL 53. Gembloux: 1980, 415-429.

1433 Coutts, J. "The Messianic Secret and the Enemies of Jesus," *SB* 2 (JSNTSS 2 1980) 37-46.

1434 Lührmann, D. "Markus 14.55-64. Christologie und Zerstörung des Tempels im Markusevangelium," *NTS* 27 (1980-81) 457-474.

1435 Flusser, D. " 'At the Right hand of Power'," *Immanuel* 14 (1982) 42-46.

1436 Vögtle, A. "Das markinische Verständnis der Tempelworte," *Die Mitte des Neuen Testaments.* Ed. U. Luz and H. Weder. (Fest. E. Schweizer). Göttingen: 1983, 362-383.

1437 Maartens, P. J. "The Son of Man as a Composite Metaphor in Mark 14:62," Ed. J. H. Petzer and P. J. Hartin. *A South African Perspective on the New Testament: Essays by South African New Testament Scholars Presented to Bruce Manning Metzger.* Leiden: 1986, 76-98.

See also 1248, 1293, 1309, 1321, 1334

XVI. Peter's Denial of Jesus

Articles

1438 Danson, J. M. ''The Fall of St. Peter,'' *ExpT* 19 (1907-08) 307-308.

1439 James, J. C. ''The Dialect of Peter's Denial,'' *ExpT* 19 (1907-08) 524.

1440 Abbott, E. A. ''The Disciple Known to the High Priest,'' *Miscellanea Evangelica*. Cambridge: 1913.

1441 Drum, W. ''The Disciple Known to the High Priest,'' *ExpT* 25 (1913-14) 381-382.

1442 Gardiner, W. D. ''The Denial of St. Peter,'' *ExpT* 26 (1914-15) 424-426.

1443 Ramsay, W. M. ''The Denials of Peter,'' *ExpT* 27 (1915-16) 296-301, 360-363, 410-413, 471-472, 540-542, 28 (1916-17) 276-281.

1444 Tindall, E. A. ''John xviii.15,'' *ExpT* 28 (1916-17) 283-284.

1445 Mayo, C. H. ''St. Peter's Token of the Cock Crow,'' *JTS* 22 (1921) 367-370.

1446 Lee, R. E. ''Luke xxii.32,'' *ExpT* 38 (1926-27) 233-234.

1447 Thomson, P. ''*epistrephō* (Luke xxii.32),'' *ExpT* 38 (1926-27) 468.

1448 Smith, P. V. ''St. Peter's Threefold Denial of Our Lord,'' *Theology* 17 (1928) 341-348.

1449 Goguel, M. ''Did Peter Deny His Lord? A Conjecture,'' *HTR* 25 (1932) 1-27.

1450 Pieper, K. ''Einige Bemerkungen zu Mt. 26,31 und Mk. 14,27,'' *BZ* 21 (1933) 320-323.

1451 Rothenaicher, F. ''Zu Mk. 14,70 und Mt. 26,73,'' *BZ* 23 (1935-36), 192-193.

1452 Thomson, J. R. "Saint Peter's Denials," *ExpT* 47 (1935-36) 381-382.

1453 Garritt, C. E. "St. Peter's Denials," *ExpT* 48 (1936-37) 43-44.

1454 Bussby, F. "St. Mark 14:72: An Aramaic Mistranslation?" *BJRL* 21 (1937) 273-274.

1455 Guyot, G. H. "Peter denies his Lord," *CBQ* 4 (1942) 111-118.

1456 Pickar, C. H. "The Prayer of Christ for Saint Peter," *CBQ* 4 (1942) 133-140.

1457 Riesenfeld, H. "The Verb *arneisthai*," *In honorem A. Fridrichsen.* ConNT 10. Lund: 1947, 207-219.

1458 Zuntz, G. "A Note on Matthew xxvi.34 and xxvi.75," *JTS* 50 (1949) 182-183.

1459 Botha, F. J. "*hymas* in Luke xxii.31," *ExpT* 64 (1952-53) 125.

1460 Lattey, C. "A Note on Cockcrow," *Scr* 6 (1953) 53-55.

1461 O'Callaghan, R. T. "Et tu aliquando conversus, St. Luke 22,32," *CBQ* 15 (1953) 305-314.

1462 Boyd, P. W. J. "Peter's Denial: Mark xiv.68, Luke xxii.57," *ExpT* 67 (1955-56) 341.

1463 Foerster, W. "Lukas 22.31f." *ZNW* 46 (1955) 129-133.

1464 Henson, B. "St. Peter's Denials of Christ," *Listener* 56 (1956) 267-268.

1465 Masson, C. "Le reniement de Pierre," *RHPR* 37 (1957) 24-35.

1466 Birdsall, J. N. "*To rhema hōs eipen auto ho Iēsous* Mk. xiv.72," *NovT* 2 (1957-58) 272-275.

1467 Krieger, N. "Der Knecht des Hohenpriesters," *NovT* 2 (1957-58) 73-74.

1468 Seitz, O. F. J. "Peter's 'Profanity.' Mark 14,71 in the light of Matthew 16,22," *SE* 1 (TU 73 1959) 516-519.

1469 Klein, G. "Die Verleugnung des Petrus," *ZTK* 58 (1961) 285-328. = *Rekonstruktion und Interpretation. Gesammelte Aufsätze zum Neuen Testament.* BEvT 50. Munich: 1969, 49-98.

1470 Kosmala, H. "The Time of the Cock-Crow," *ASTI* 2 (1963) 118-120.

1471 Schwank, B. "Petrus verleugnet Jesus," *Sein und Sendung* 29 (1964) 51-65.

1472 Kosnetter, J. "Zur Geschichtlichkeit der Verleugnung Petri," *Dienst an der Lehre* (Fest. F. K. König). Vienna: 1965, 127-143.

1473 Linnemann, E. "Die Verleugnung des Petrus," *ZTK* 63 (1966) 1-32.

1474 Zeck, P. R. "Fall und Wiederaufstehen eines Jüngers. Passionsbetrachtung zu Mk 14,66-72," *BuL* 7 (1966) 51-57.

1475 Kosmala, H. "The Time of the Cock-Crow (11)," *ASTI* 6 (1967-68) 132-134.

1476 Merkel, H. "Peter's Curse," *The Trial of Jesus*. Ed. E. Bammel, SBT 2d. ser. 13. Naperville, IL: 1970, 66-71.

1477 Lee, G. M. "Mark 14,72: *epibalon eklaien*," *Bib* 53 (1972) 411-412.

1478 Lampe, G. W. H. "St. Peter's Denial," *BJRL* 55 (1973) 346-368.

1479 Wilcox, M. "The Denial Sequence in Mark 14,26-31, 66-72," *NTS* 20 (1973-74) 445-452.

1480 Pesch, R. "Die Verleugnung des Petrus. Eine Studie zu Mk. 14,54. 66-72," *Neues Testament und Kirche*. Ed. J. Gnilka (Fest. R. Schnackenburg). Freiburg: 1974, 42-62.

1481 Neirynck, F. "The 'Other Disciple' in Jn. 18,15-16," *ETL* 51 (1975) 113-141.

1482 Dewey, K. E. "Peter's Curse and Cursed Peter (Mark 14:53-54, 66-72)," *The Passion in Mark: Studies on Mark 14-16*. Ed. W. H. Kelber. Philadelphia: 1976, 96-114.

1483 Ernst, J. "Noch einmal: Die Verleugnung Jesu durch Petrus," *Petrus und Papst*. Ed. A. Brandenburg and H. J. Urban. Münster: 1977, 43-62.

1484 Walter, N. "Die Verleugnung des Petrus," *Theologische Versuche* Ed. J. Rogge and G. Schille. Berlin: 1977, 45-62.

1485 Fortna, R. T. "Jesus and Peter at the High Priest's House: A Test Case for the Question of the Relation Between Mark's and John's Gospels," *NTS* 24 (1978) 371-382.

1486 Gewalt, D. "Die Verleugnung des Petrus," *LingBib* 43 (1978) 113-144.

1487 Wenham, J. W. "How Many Cock-Crowings? The Problem of Harmonistic Text-Variants," *NTS* 25 (1978-79) 523-525.

1488 Brady, D. "The Alarm to Peter in Mark's Gospel," *JSNT* 4 (1979) 42-57.

1489 Brunet, G. "Et aussitôt le coq chanta," *Cahiers du Cercle Ernst Renan* 27 (1979) 9-12.

1490 Dewey, K. E. "Peter's Denial Reexamined: John's Knowledge of Mark's Gospel," *SBLASP* (1979), 1:109-112.

1491 Dassman, E. "Die Szene Christus—Petrus mit der Hahn," *Pietas.* Ed. E. Dassman and K. S. Frank (Fest. B. Kotting). JAC 8. Münster: 1980. 510-511.

1492 Gerhardsson, B. "Confession and Denial before Men: Observations on Matt. 26:57-27:2," *JSNT* (1981) 46-66.

1493 Evans, C. A. " 'Peter Warming Himself': The Problem of an Editorial Seam," *JBL* 100 (1982) 245-249.

1494 Derrett, J. D. M. "The Reason for the Cock-Crowings," *NTS* 29 (1983) 142-144.

1495 Murray, G. "Saint Peter's Denials," *DownRev* 103 (1985) 296-298.

1496 LaVerdiere, E. A. "Peter Broke Down and Began to Cry," *Emmanuel* 92 (1986) 70-73.

1497 Soards, M. L. " 'And the Lord Turned and Looked Straight at Peter': Understanding Luke 22,61," *Bib* 67 (1986) 518-519.

1498 Boomershine, T. E. "Peter's Denial as Polemic or Confession: The Implications of Media Criticism for Biblical Hermeneutics," *Semeia* 39 (1987) 47-68.

1499 Fox, R. "Peter's Denial in Mark's Gospel," *Bible Today* 25 (1987) 298-303.

See also 0292, 0346

XVII. Judas' Death in Matthew

Articles

1500 Hatch, H. R. "The Old Testament Quotation in Matthew 27:9, 10," *Biblical World* 1 (1893) 345-354

1501 Harris, J. R. "Did Judas Really Commit Suicide?" *AJT* 4 (1900) 490-513.

1502 Bernard, J. H. "The Death of Judas," *Exp* 6th ser. 9 (1904) 422-430.

1503 Pfättisch, J. M. "Der Besitzer des Blutackers," *BZ* 7 (1909) 303-311.

1504 Sigwalt, C. "Eine andere Erläuterung von dem 'Besitzer des Blutackers'," *BZ* 9 (1911) 399.

1505 Munro, J. I. "The Death of Judas (Matt. xxvii.3-8; Acts 1:18-19)," *ExpT* 24 (1912-13) 235-236.

1506 Harris, J. R. "St. Luke's Version of the Death of Judas," *American Journal of Theology* 18 (1914) 127-131.

1507 Knox, A. D. "The Death of Judas," *JTS* 25 (1923-24) 289-290.

1508 Lake, K. "The Death of Judas," *The Beginnings of Christianity. Part 1. The Acts of the Apostles*. Ed. F. J. Foakes Jackson and K. Lake. New York: 1932, V:22-30.

1509 Herber, J. "La mort de Judas," *RHR* 129 (1945) 47-56.

1510 Sutcliffe, E. F. "Matthew 27,9," *JTS* 3 (1952) 227-228.

1511 Bauer, J. "Judas Schicksal und Selbstmord," *BLit* 20 (1952-53) 210-213.

1512 Benoit, P. "La mort de Judas," *Synoptische Studien* (Fest. A. Wikenhauser). Munich: 1953, 1-19. = *Exégèse et Théologie*. Paris: 1961, 1:340-362. Eng. trans. "The Death of Judas," *Jesus and Gospel*. Trans. B. Weatherhead. New York: 1973, 188-207.

1513 Betz, O. "The Dichotomized Servant and the End of Judas Iscariot," *RQ* 5 (1964) 43-58.

1514 Jervell, J. "The Field of Jesus Blood. Mt. 27,3-10," *NorTT* 69 (1968) 59-73.

1515 Reiner, E. "Thirty Pieces of Silver," *Essays in Memory of E. A. Speiser*. New Haven: 1968, 186-190.

1516 Senior, D. P. "The Fate of the Betrayer. A Redactional Study of Matthew XXVII,3-10," *ETL* 48 (1972) 372-426.

1517 Van Unnik, W. C. "The Death of Judas in Saint Matthew's Gospel," *ATR* sup. ser. 3 (1974) 44-57.

1518 Senior, D. P. "A Case Study in Matthean Creativity. Matthew 27:3-10," *BR* 19 (1974) 23-36.

1519 Zehrer, F. "Zum Judasproblem," *TPQ* 121 (1973) 259-264.

1520 Manns, F. "Un midrash chrétien: le récit de la mort de Judas," *RSR* 54 (1980) 197-203.

1521 Derrett, J. D. M. "Miscellanea: a Pauline Pun and Judas' Punishment," *ZNW* 72 (1981) 131-133.

1522 Luke, K. "The Thirty Pieces of Silver," *Indian Theological Studies* 19 (1982) 15-22.

1523 Upton, J. A. "The Potter's Field and the Death of Judas," *Conc Journ* 8 (1982) 213-219.

1524 Moo, D. J. "Tradition and Old Testament in Matt. 27:3-10," *Gospel Perspectives* III. Ed. R. T. France and D. Wenham (Sheffield: 1983) 157-175.

1525 Roquefort, D. "Judas: une figure de la perversion," *ETR* 58 (1983) 501-513.

1526 Mencken, M. J. J. "The References to Jeremiah in the Gospel according to Matthew (Mt 2,17; 16,14; 27,9)," *ETL* 60 (1984) 5-24.

1527 Schwarz, W. "Die Doppelbedeutung des Judastodes," *BLit* 57 (1984) 227-233.

1528 Stein-Schneider, H. "A la recherche du Judas historique. Une enquête exégétique à la lumière des textes de l'Ancien Testament et des Logia," *ETR* 60 (1985) 403-429.

1529 Desautels, L. "La Mort de Judas (Mt 27,3-10; Ac 1,15-16)," *ScES* 38 (1986) 221-239.

XVIII. The Trial before Pilate

Books

1530 Mommsen, T. *Römisches Strafrecht*. Leipzig: 1899.

1531 James, E. H. *The Trial Before Pilate*. 2 vols. Concord: 1909.

1532 Regnault, H. *Une province procuratorienne an début de l'empire romain. Le procès de Jésus-Christ*. Paris: 1909.

1533 Kastner, K. *Jesus vor Pilatus. Ein Beitrag zur Leidensgeschichte des Herrn*. Münster: 1912.

1534 Juechen, A. V. *Jesus und Pilatus. Eine Untersuchung über das Verhältnis von Gottesreich und Weltreich im Anschluss an Johannes 18,v.28-19,v.16*. Munich: 1941.

1535 Stevenson, G. H. *Roman Provincial Administration*. Oxford: 1949.

1536 Sherwin-White, A. N. *Roman Society and Roman Law in the New Testament*. Oxford: 1963.

1537 Caillois, R. *Pontius Pilate*. New York: 1963.

1538 Colin, J. *Les villes libres de l'Orient greco-romain et l'envoi au supplice par acclamations populaires*. Bruxelles/Berchem: 1965.

1539 Lernet-Holenia, A. *Pilatus. Ein Komplex*. Vienna: 1967.

1540 Speidel, K. A. *Das Urteil des Pilatus. Berichte und Bilder zur Passion Jesu*. Stuttgart: 1976.

1541 Lemonon, J. P. *Pilate et le gouvernement de la Judée. Textes et Monuments*. Paris: 1981.

Articles

1542 Perles, J. ''Bileam — Jesus und Pontius Pilatus,'' *MGWJ* 21 (1872) 266-267.

1543 Cox, S. "A Day in Pilate's Life," *Exp* 2d ser, 8 (1884) 107-128.

1544 Roberts, A. "On the Proper Rendering of *ekathisen* in John xix.13," *ExpT* 4th ser. 8 (1893) 296-308.

1545 Watson, R. A. "They Cried the More," *Exp* 4th ser. 8 (1893) 471-472.

1546 Wendland, P. "Jesu als Saturnalienkönig," *Hermes* 33 (1898) 175-179.

1547 Bacon, B. W. "Exegetical Notes: John 19:17-20," *BW* 13 (1899) 423-425.

1548 Brüll, A. "Die Ergreifung und Überlieferung Jesu an Pilatus," *TQ* 83 (1901) 161-186; 396-411.

1549 Porteous, J. "Note on John xix.11: 'The Greater Sin'," *ExpT* 15 (1903-04) 428-429.

1550 Reich, H. "Der König mit der Dornenkrone," *Neue Jahrbücher für das klassische Altertum, Geschichte und Deutsche Literatur* 13 (1904) 705-733.

1551 Eager, A. R. "The Greater Sin. A Note on St. John xix.11," *Exp* 6th ser. (1905) 33-40.

1552 Van Berber, H. "Das Prätorium des Pilatus," *TQ* 87 (1905) 209-230.

1553 Vollmer, H. "Der König mit der Dornenkrone," *ZNW* 6 (1905) 194-198.

1554 Grey, H. G. "A Suggestion on St. John xix.14," *Exp* 7th ser. 2 (1906) 451-454.

1555 Streeter, B. H. "On the Trial of our Lord before Herod," *Studies in the Synoptic Problem by Members of the University of Oxford.* Ed. W. Sanday. Oxford: 1911, 229-234.

1556 Corssen, P. "*Ekathisen epi Bēmatos*," *ZNW* 15 (1914) 338-340.

1557 Wood, H. G. "A Mythical Incident in the Trial of Jesus," *ExpT* 28 (1916-17) 459-460.

1558 Tolman, H. "A Possible Restoration from a Middle Persian Source of the Answer of Jesus to Pilate's Inquiry: "What is Truth?" *JAOS* 39 (1919) 55-57.

1559 Baldensperger, G. "Il à rendu témoignage devant Ponce Pilate," *RHPR* 2 (1922) 1-25; 95-117.

1560 Steele, J. A. "The Pavement," *ExpT* 34 (1922-23) 562-563.

1561 Flourney, P. P. "What Frightened Pilate?" *BSac* 82 (1925) 314-320.

1562 Thibault, R. "La résponse de Notre Seigneur à Pilate (Jean 19,11)," *NRT* 54 (1927) 208-211.

1563 Lattey, C. "The Praetorium of Pilate," *JTS* 31 (1929-30) 180-182.

1564 Cooke, H. P. "Christ Crucified—and by Whom?" *HibJ* 29 (1930-31) 61-74.

1565 Merlier, O. "*SY LEGEIS, HOTI BASILEUS EIMI* (Jean 18,37)," *Revue des Études Grecques* 45 (1933) 204-209.

1566 Chaming-Pearce, M. "The Ethics of a Kingdom not of this World," *HibJ* 34 (1935-36) 45-56.

1567 Kingdon, H. P. "Had the Crucifixion a Political Significance?" *HeyJ* 35 (1936-37), 556-567.

1568 Nicklin, T. "Thou sayest," *ExpT* 51 (1939-40) 155.

1569 Fluegel, H. "Pilatus vor Christus," *Eckart* 16 (1940) 58-63.

1570 Schlier, H. "Jesus und Pilatus nach dem Johannesevangelium," *Christus, des Gesetzes Ende*. Munich: 1940, 28-49.

1571 Delbrück, R. "Antiquarisches zu den Verspottungen Jesu," *ZNW* 41 (1942) 124-125.

1572 Carver, W. O. "The Christian Message is Christ," *RevExp* 40 (1943) 286-303.

1573 Ehrhardt, A. "Was Pilate a Christian?" *CQR* 137 (1944) 157-167.

1574 Liberty, S. "The Importance of Pontius Pilate in Creed and Gospel," *JTS* 45 (1944) 38-56.

1575 Derwacter, F. W. "The Modern Translators and John 19:13: Is Is It 'Sat' or 'Seated,' " *Classical Journal* 40 (1944-45) 24-28.

1576 Fascher, E. "Das Weib des Pilatus," *TLZ* 72 (1947) 201-203.

1577 Campenhausen, H. von. "Zum Verständnis von Joh. 19,11," *TLZ* 73 (1948) 387-392.

1578 Davies, D. R. "What is Truth?" *LondQR* 173 (1948) 112-117.

1579 Dekkers, R. "Jésus et ses disciples devant la loi romaine," *Revue de l'Université de Bruxelles 1* (1948-49) 350-352.

1580 Harrison, E. F. "Jesus and Pilate," *BSac* 105 (1948) 307-319.

1581 Oepke, A. "Noch einmal das Weib des Pilatus; Fragment einer Dämonologie," *TLZ* 73 (1948) 743-747.

1582 Bammel, E. "Syrian Coinage and Pilate," *JJS* 2 (1951) 108-110.

1583 Jones, A. H. M. "The Imperium of Augustus," *JRS* 41 (1951) 112-119.

1584 Bammel, E. "*Philos tou Kaisaras*," *TLZ* 77 (1952) 205-210.

1585 Benoit, P. "Prétoire, Lithostroton et Gabbatha," *RB* 59 (1952) 531-550. Eng. trans.: "Praetorium, Lithostroton and Gabbatha," *Jesus and Gospel*. Trans. B. Weatherhead. New York: 1973, 167-188.

1586 Bonsirven, J. "Hora talmudica. La notation chronologique de Jean 19,4 aurait-elle un sens symbolique," *Bib* 33 (1952) 511-515.

1587 Cantinat, J. "Jésus devant Pilate," *VSpir* 86 (1952) 227-247.

1588 Hart, H. St. J. "The Crown of Thorns in John 19:2,5," *JTS* 3 (1952) 66-73.

1589 Vincent, L. H. "Le Lithostrotos évangélique," *RB* 59 (1952) 513-530.

1590 Ammon, W. V. "Das Strafverfahren gegen Jesus von Nazareth," *NELKB* (1953) 69-72.

1591 Bonner, C. "The Crown of Thorns," *HTR* 46 (1953) 47-49.

1592 Goodenough, E. R. and Welles, C. B. "The Crown of Acanthus(?)," *HTR* 46 (1953) 241-242.

1593 Kurfess, A. "*EKATHISEN EPI BĒMATOS* (Jo. 19,13)," *Bib* 34 (1953) 271.

1594 Blinzler, J. "Der Entschied des Pilatus—Exekutions Befehl oder Todesurteil?" *MTZ* 5 (1954) 171-184.

1595 Smallwood, E. M. "The Date of the Dismissal of Pontius Pilate from Judaea," *JJS* 5 (1954) 12-21.

1596 Chilton, C. W. "The Roman Law of Treason Under the Early Principiate," *JRS* 45 (1955) 73-81.

1597 Schlier, H. "Jesus und Pilatus nach dem Johannesevangelium," *Die Zeit der Kirche. Exegetische Aufsätze und Vorträge*. Freiburg: 1956, 56-74.

1598 Lohse, E. "Die römischen Statthalter in Jerusalem," *ZDPV* 74 (1958) 69-78.

1599 Blank, J. "Der Verhandlung vor Pilatus, Joh. xviii 28-ixx 16 im Lichte Johanneischer Theologie," *BZ* 3 (1959) 60-81.

1600 Rogers, R. S. "Treason in the Early Empire," *JRS* 49 (1959) 90-94.

1601 de la Potterie, I. "Jésus Roi et Juge d'après Jo. ixx 13," *Bib* 41 (1960) 217-247. = de la Potterie, I. "Jesus King and Judge acc. to Jn. 19,13," *Scr* 13 (1961) 97-111.

1602 Haenchen, E. "Jesus vor Pilatus (Joh. xviii 28-ix 15)," *TLZ* 85 (1960) 93-102. = *Gott und Mensch*. Tübingen: 1965, 144-156.

1603 Irmscher, J. "*sy legeis* (Mark xv.2 — Matt. xxvii.11-Luke xxiii.3)," *Studii Classice* 2 (1960) 151-158.

1604 Jones, A. H. M. "Procurators and Prefects," *Studies in Roman Government and Law*. Oxford: 1960, 115-125.

1605 Verdam, P. J. "Sanhedrin and Gabbatha," *Free University Quarterly* 7 (1960-61) 259-287.

1606 Braumann, G. "Mk. 15,2-5 und Mk. 14,55-64," *ZNW* 52 (1961) 273-278.

1607 Mollat, D. "Jésus devant Pilate (Jean 18,28-38)," *BVC* 39 (1961) 23-31.

1608 Becq, J. "Ponce Pilata et la mort de Jésus," *BTS* 57 (1963) 2-7.

1609 O'Rourke, J. J. "Two Notes on St. John's Gospel," *CBQ* 25 (1963) 124-128.

1610 Schwank, B. "Pilatus begegnet dem Christus (18,28-38a)," *Sein und Sendung* 29 (1964) 100-112.

1611 Schwank, B. "Der Dornengekrönte (18,38b-19,7)," *Sein und Sendung* 29 (1964) 148-160.

1612 Schwank, B. "Der königliche Richter (19,8-16a)," *Sein und Sendung* 29 (1964) 196-208.

1613 Trilling, W. "Der Prozess vor Pilatus: 27,15-26," *Das Wahre Israel*. 3d. ed. SANT 10. Munich: 1964, 66-74.

1614 Colin, J. "Sur le procés de Jésus devant Pilate et le peuple," *Revue des Études Anciennes* 67 (1965) 159-164.

1615 Sherwin-White, A. N. "The Trial of Christ," *Historicity and Chronology in the New Testament*. Ed. D. Nineham. Oxford: 1965, 97-116.

1616 Boismard, M. E. "La royauté universelle du Christ (Jn. 18, 35-37)," *AsSeign* 88 (1966) 33-45.

1617 Garnsey, P. "The Criminal Jurisdiction of Governors," *JRS* 58 (1968) 51-59.

1618 Schlier, H. "The State according to the New Testament," *The Relevance of the New Testament*. Trans. W. J. O'Hara. New York: 1968, 215-238.

1619 Horvath, T. "Why was Jesus Brought to Pilate," *NovT* 11 (1969) 174-184.

1620 Wead, D. W. "We have a Law," *NovT* 11 (1969) 185-189.

1621 Winter, P. "The Trial of Jesus as a Rebel against Rome," *Jewish Quarterly* 16 (1968) 31-37.

1622 Allen, J. E. "Why Pilate?" *The Trial of Jesus*. Ed. E. Bammel. SBT 2d ser. 13. Naperville, IL: 1970, 78-83.

1623 Burkill, T. A. "The Condemnation of Jesus: A Critique of Sherwin-White's Thesis," *NovT* 12 (1970) 321-342.

1624 Hahn, F. "Der Prozess Jesu nach dem Johannesevangelium. Eine redaktionsgeschichtliche Untersuchung," EKKNT Vorarbeiten Heft 2. Zurich: 1970, 23-96.

1625 Quinn, J. F. "The Pilate Sequence in the Gospel of Matthew," *DunRev* 10 (1970) 154-177.

1626 Benoit, P. "L'Antonia d'Hérode le grand et le Forum Oriental d'Aelia Capitolina," *HTR* 64 (1971) 135-167.

1627 Marin, L. "Jésus devant Pilate. Essai d'analyse structurale," *Langages* 22 (1971) 51-74; = "Jesus vor Pilatus. Versuch einer Strukturanalyse," *Erzählende Semiotik nach Berichten der Bibel*. Ed. C. Chabrol. Munich: 1973, 87-122.

1628 Sobosan, J. G. "The Trial of Jesus," *JES* 10 (1973) 72-91.

1629 Escande, J. "Jésus devant Pilate. Jean 18,28-19,24," *Foi et Vie* 73 (1974) 66-81.

1630 Jaubert, A. "La comparution devant Pilate selon Jean 18,28-19,16," *Foi et Vie* 73 (1974) 3-12.

1631 Barnett, P. W. " 'Under Tiberias All Was Quiet'," *NTS* 21 (1974-75) 564-571.

1632 Schnackenburg, R. "Die Eccehomo Szene und der Menschensohn," *Jesus und der Menschensohn*. Ed. R. Pesch and R. Schnackenburg (Fest. A. Vögtle). Freiburg: 1975, 371-386.

1633 Wijngaards, J. N. M. "The Awe-Inspiring Reality of Christ's Silence," *Indian Journal of Theology* 24 (1975) 132-142.

1634 Ford, J. M. " 'Crucify him, crucify him' and the Temple Scroll," *ExpT* 87 (1976) 274-278.

1635 Foulon-Piganiol, C. L. "Le rôle du peuple dans le procés de Jésus. Une hypothèse juridique et théologique," *NRT* 98 (1976) 627-637.

1636 Overstreet, L. "Roman Law and the Trial of Christ," *BSac* 135 (1978) 323-332.

1637 Derrett, J. D. M. " 'Have nothing to do with that just man!' (Matt. 27,19). Haggadah and the Account of the Passion," *Downside Review* 97 (1979) 308-315.

1638 Escande, J. "Judas et Pilate prisonniers d'une même structure (Mt 27,1-26)," *Foi et Vie* 78 (1979) 92-100.

1639 Janssen, L. " 'Superstitio' and Persecution of the Christians,'' *VC* 33 (1979) 131-159.

1640 Alegre, C. "My Kingdom is not of This World,'' *TD* 19 (1981) 231-235.

1641 Delorme, J. "Le procés de Jésus ou la parole risquée (Lc. 22, 54-23,25),'' *RSR* 69 (1981) 123-146.

1642 Houlden, J. L. "John 19:5: 'And he said to them, Behold, the man','' *ExpT* 92 (1981) 148-149.

1643 Zabala, A. M. "The Enigma of John 19:13 Reconsidered (A Survey of the Contemporary Discussion and a Suggestion,'' *SEAJT* 23 (1982) 1-10.

1644 Charbonneau, A. "L'interrogatoire de Jésus, d'après la facture interne de Jn 18,12-17,'' *ScEs* 35 (1983) 191-210.

1645 Ehrman, B. D. "Jesus' Trial Before Pilate: John 18:28-19:16,'' *BTB* 13 (1983) 124-131.

1646 Rensberger, D. "The Politics of John: The Trial of Jesus in the Fourth Gospel,'' *JBL* 103 (1983) 395-411.

1647 Robert, R. "Pilate a-t-il fait de Jésus un jude? *ekathisen epi bēmatos* (Jean, xix,13),'' *RevThom* 83 (1983) 275-287.

1648 Schwarz, D. R. "Josephus and Philo on Pontius Pilate,'' *The Jerusalem Cathedral* 3 (1983) 26-45.

1649 Suggit, J. "John 19:5: 'Behold the man','' *ExpT* 94 (1983) 333-334.

1650 Bammel, E. "The trial before Pilate,'' *Jesus and the Politics of His Day*. Ed. E. Bammel and C. F. D. Moule. Cambridge: 1984, 415-452.

1651 Schneider, G. "The political charge against Jesus (Luke 23:2),'' *Jesus and the Politics of His Day*. Ed. E. Bammel and C. F. D. Moule. Cambridge: 1984, 403-412.

1652 Flusser, D. "What was the Original Meaning of *Ecce Homo?*'' *Immanuel* 19 (1984-85) 30-40.

1653 Dewailly, L.-M. " 'D'ou es tu?' (Jean 19,9),'' *RB* 92 (1985) 481-496.

1654 Genuyt, F. "La comparution de Jésus devant Pilate. Analyse semiotique de Jean 18,28-19,16,'' *RSR* 73 (1985) 133-146.

1655 Bammel, E. "Pilatus und Kaiphas' Absetzung,'' *Judaica*. Tübingen: 1986, 1:51-58.

1656 Charbonneau, A. " 'Qu'as-tu fait' et 'D'oú es-tu?' Le procés de Jésus chez Jean (18,28-19,16a) (2eme partie),'' *ScEs* 38 (1986) 317-329.

1657 Imbert, J. "Le procés de Jésus," *RICP* 19 (1986) 53-66.

1658 McGing, B. C. "The Governorship of Pontius Pilate: Messiahs and Sources," *Proceedings of the Irish Biblical Association* 10 (1986) 55-71.

1659 Orr, E. "Wer war die Frau des Pilatus? Eine Geschichte für heute," *GuL* 59 (1986) 104-106.

1660 Riesner, R. "Das Prätorium des Pilatus," *BK* 41 (1986) 34-37.

1661 Hill, D. " 'My Kingdom is not of this World' (Jn 18.36): Conflict and Christian Existence in the World according to the Fourth Gospel," *IBS* 9 (1987) 54-62.

1662 Staats, R. K. "Pontius Pilatus im Bekenntnis der frühen Kirche," *ZTK* 84 (1987) 493-513.

1663 Robbins, V. K. "The Crucifixion and the Speech of Jesus," *Forum* 4 (1988) 33-46.

See also 0220, 0233, 0248, 0254, 0362, 0385, 0403, 0405, 0418, 0420, 0421, 0432, 0572, 1246, 1269, 1291, 1300, 1309, 1320, 1352, 1383, 1684-1700, 1736, 2121-2124

XIX. The Hearing Before Herod

Books

1664 Blinzler, J. *Herodes Antipas und Jesus Christus*. Stuttgart: 1947.

1665 Harlow, V. E. *The Destroyer of Jesus: The Story of Herod Antipas. Tetrarch of Galilee*. Oklahoma City: 1954.

1666 Hoehner, H. W. *Herod Antipas* SNTSMS 17. Cambridge: 1972.

Articles

1667 Verrall, A. W. "Christ Before Herod," *JTS* 10 (1910) 321-353.

1668 Dibelius, M. "Herodes und Pilatus," *ZNW* 16 (1915) 113-126 = *Botschaft und Geschichte*. Tübingen: 1953, 1:278-292.

1669 Bornhäuser, K. "Die Beteiligung des Herodes am Prozesse Jesu," *NKZ* 40 (1929) 714-718.

1670 Joüon, P. "Luc 23,11: *esthēta lampran*," *RSR* 26 (1936) 80-85.

1671 Harlow, V. E. "The Destroyer of Jesus; the Story of Herod Antipas," *RHPR* 26 (1956) 85-86.

1672 Tyson, J. B. "Jesus and Herod Antipas," *JBL* 79 (1960) 239-246.

1673 Bruce, F. F. "Herod Antipas, Tetrarch of Galilee and Peraea," *ALUOS* 5 (1963) 6-23.

1674 Hoehner, H. W. "Why did Pilate hand Jesus over to Antipas?" *The Trial of Jesus*. Ed. E. Bammel. SBT 2d ser. 13. Naperville, IL: 1970, 84-90.

1675 Corbin, M. "Jésus devant Hérode. Lecture de Luc. 23,6-12," *Christus* 25 (1978) 190-197.

1676 Müller, K. "Jesus vor Herodes. Eine redaktionsgeschichtliche Untersuchung zu Lk. 23,6-12," *Zur Geschichte des Urchristentums*. Ed. G. Dautzenberg, H. Merklein, and K. Müller. QD 87. Freiburg/Basel/Vienna: 1979, 111-141.

1677 Buck, E. "The Function of the Pericope 'Jesus before Herod' in the Passion Narrative of Luke," *Wort in der Zeit*. Ed. W. Haubeck and M. Bachmann (Fest. K. H. Rengstorf). Leiden: 1980, 165-178.

1678 Soards, M. L. "The Silence of Jesus Before Herod," *AusBR* 33 (1985) 41-45.

1679 Soards, M. L. "Tradition, Composition and Theology in Luke's Account of Jesus Before Herod Antipas," *Bib* 66 (1985) 344-364.

1680 Soards, M. L. " 'Herod Antipas' Hearing in Luke 23:8," *BT* 37 (1986) 146-147.

1681 Manus, C. U. "The Universalism of Luke and the Motif of Reconciliation in Luke 23:6-13," *African Journal of Theology* 16 (1987) 121-135.

1682 Parker, P. "Herod Antipas and the Death of Jesus," *Jesus, the Gospels, And the Church: Essays in Honor of William R. Farmer*. Ed. E. P. Sanders. Macon, Ga.: 1987.

1683 Soards, M. L. "A Literary Analysis of the Origin and Purpose of Luke's Account of the Mockery of Jesus," *BZ* 31 (1987) 110-115.

XX. Barabbas

Articles

1684 Wratislaw, A. H. "The Scapegoat — Barabbas," *ExpT* 3 (1891-92) 400-403.

1685 Merkel, J. "Die Begnadigung am Passafest," *ZNW* 6 (1905) 293-316.

1686 Husband, R. W. "The Pardoning of Prisoners by Pilate," *AJT* 21 (1917) 110-116.

1687 Langdon, S. "The Release of the Prisoner at the Passover," *ExpT* 29 (1918) 328-330.

1688 Couchoud, L. and Stahl, R. "Jesus Barabbas," *HibJ* 25 (1927) 26-42.

1689 Chavel, C. B. "The Releasing of a Prisoner on the Eve of Passover in Ancient Jerusalem," *JBL* 60 (1941) 273-278.

1690 Davis, W. H. "Origen's Comment on Matthew 27:17," *RevExp* 39 (1942) 65-67.

1691 Rigg, H. A. "Barabbas," *JBL* 64 (1945) 417-456.

1692 Twomey, J. J. "Barabbas Was a Robber," *Scr* 8 (1956) 115-119.

1693 Dunkerley, R. "Was Barabbas also called Jesus?" *ExpT* 74 (1962-63) 126.

1694 Nevius, R. "A Reply to Dr. Dunkerley," *ExpT* 74 (1962-63) 225.

1695 Bajsic, A. "Pilatus, Jesus und Barabbas," *Bib* 48 (1967) 7-28.

1696 Maccoby, H. Z. "Jesus and Barabbas," *NTS* 16 (1969-70) 55-60.

1697 Davies, S. L. "Who is Called Bar Abbas?" *NTS* 27 (1980-81) 260-262.

1698 Merritt, R. L. "Jesus Barabbas and the Paschal Pardon," *JBL* 104 (1985) 57-68.

See also 0200

XXI. The Cry His Blood
Be Upon Us
and Our Children

Books

1699 Kampling, R. *Das Blut Christi und die Juden: Mt 27,25 bei den lateinischsprächigen christlichen Autoren bis zu Leo dem Grossem*. NTAbh 16. Aschendorff/Münster: 1984.

1700 Mora, V. *Le refus d' Israel. Matthieu 27,25*. LD 124. Paris: 1986.

Articles

1701 Joüon, P. "Notes philologiques sur les Évangiles.—Matthieu 27,25," *RSR* 8 (1928) 349-350.

1702 Rabinowitz, J. J. "Demotic Papyri of the Ptolemaic Period and Jewish Sources, 'on the Head of,' " *VT* 7 (1957), 398-399.

1703 Reventlow, H. "Sein Blut komme über sein Haupt," *VT* 10 (1960) 311-327.

1704 Fitzmyer, J. A. "Anti-Semitism and the Cry of 'All the People' (Mt. 27:26)," *TS* 26 (1965) 667-671.

1705 Schelkle, K. H. "Die 'Selbstverfluchung' Israels nach Mt. 27:23-25," *Antijudäismus in Neuen Testament? Ed. W. Eckert. Munich: 1967, 148-156.

1706 Kosmala, H. " 'His Blood on Us and on Our Children' (The Background of Matt. 27,24-25)," *ASTI* (1968-69) 94-126.

1707 Sanders, W. "Das Blut Jesu and die Juden. Gedanken zu Matth. 27,25," *US* 27 (1972) 168-171.

1708 Frankemölle, H. "27,25: *pas ho laos*," *Jahwebund und Kirche Christi*. NTAbh 10. Münster: 1973, 204-211.

1709 Bowman, J. "The Significance of Mt. 27:25," *Milla wa-Milla* 14 (1974) 26-31.

1710 Haacker, K. " 'Sein Blut über uns': Erwägungen zu Matthäus 27,25," *Kirche und Israel* 1 (1986) 47-50.

1711 Lovsky, F. "Comment comprendre 'Son sang sur nous et nos enfants,' " *ETR* 62 (1987) 343-362.

See also 0260

XXII. Crucifixion

Books

1712 Degen, P. *Das Kreuz als Strafwerkzeug und Strafe der Alten.* Aachen: 1872.

1713 Fulda, H. *Das Kreuz und die Kreuzigung. Eine antiquarische Untersuchung nebst Nachweis der vielen seit Lipsius verbreiteten Irrthumer.* Breslau: 1878.

1714 Jeremias, J. *Golgotha.* Leipzig: 1926.

1715 Barbet, P. *Le Passion de N.-S. Jésus Christ selon le Chirurgien.* Issoudun: 1953. = *A Doctor at Calvary.* Trans. By The Earl of Wicklow. Garden City, NY: 1963.

1716 Hengel, M. "*Mors turpissma crucis.* Die Kreuzigung in der antiken Welt und die 'Torheit' des 'Wortes vom Kreuz,'" *Rechtfertigung.* Ed. J. Friedrich, W. Pöhlmann, and P. Stuhlmacher (Fest. E. Käsemann). Tübingen: 1976, 125-184. = *Crucifixion.* Trans. J. Bowden. Philadelphia: 1977.

1717 Martin, E. L. *The Place of Christ's Crucifixion: Its Discovery and Significance.* Pasadena: 1984.

Articles

1718 Buchler, A. "Die Todesstrafen der Bibel und der jüdisch-nachbiblischen Zeit," *MGWJ* 50 (1906) 542-562, 664-691.

1719 Hewitt, J. W. "The Use of Nails in the Crucifixion," *HTR* 25 (1932) 29-46.

1720 Holzmeister, U. "Crux Domini eiusque crucifixio ex Archaeologia Romana illustrantur," *VD* 14 (1934) 149-155; 216-220; 241-249; 257-263.

1721 Rosenblatt, S. "The Crucifixion of Jesus from the Standpoint of Pharisaic Law," *JBL* 75 (1956) 315-321.

1722 Fischer, H. "Die öffene Kreuzhaltung im Rechtsritual," *GRSS* 3 (Fest. A. Steinwenter). Graz/Cologne: 1958, 9-57.

1723 Bammel, E. "Crucifixion as a Punishment in Palestine," *The Trial of Jesus*. Ed. E. Bammel, SBT 2d. ser. 13. Naperville, IL.: 1970, 162-165.

1724 Blinzler, J. "The Jewish Punishment of Stoning in the New Testament Period," *The Trial of Jesus*. Ed. E. Bammel, SBT 2d. ser. 13. Naperville, IL.: 1970, 147-161.

1725 Haas, N. "Anthropological Observations on the Skeletal Remains from Giv'at ha-Mivtar," *IEJ* 20 (1970) 38-59.

1726 Naveh, J. "The Ossuary Inscriptions from Giv'at ha-Mivtar," *IEJ* 20 (1970) 33-37.

1727 Tzaferis, V. "Jewish Tombs at and near Giv'at ha-Mivtar, Jerusalem," *IEJ* 20 (1970) 18-32.

1728 Arnold, M. "La crucifixion dans le droit romain," *BTS* 133 (1971) 4.

1729 Fransen, I. "L'historien Flavius-Josephe et le supplice de la croix," *BTS* 133 (1971) 5.

1730 Yadin, Y. "Pesher Nahum (4QpNahum) Reconsidered," *IEJ* 21 (1971) 1-12.

1731 Baumgarten, J. M. "Does the *tlh* in the Temple Scroll Refer to Crucifixion?" *JBL* 91 (1972) 472-481.

1732 Charlesworth, J. H. "Jesus and Jehohanan: An Archaeological Note on Crucifixion," *ExpT* 84 (1973) 147-150.

1733 Vogt, J. "Crucificux etiam pro nobis. Historische Anmerkungen zum Kreuzestod," *IKZ* 2 (1973) 186-191.

1734 Yadin, Y. "Epigraphy and Crucifixion," *IEJ* 23 (1973) 19-22.

1735 Kuhn, H.-W. "Jesus als Gekreuzigter in der frühchristlichen Verkündigung bis zur Mitte des 2. Jahrhunderts," *ZTK* 72 (1975) 1-46.

1736 Ford, J. M. " 'Crucify Him, Crucify Him,' and the Temple Scroll," *ExpT* 87 (1975-76) 275-278.

1737 Möller-Christensen, V. "Skeletal Remains from Giv'at ha-Mivtar," *IEJ* 26 (1976) 35-38.

1738 Fitzmyer, J. A. "Crucifixion in Ancient Palestine," *CBQ* 40 (1978) 493-513.

1739 Kuhn, H.-W. "Zum Gekreuzigten von Giv'at ha-Mivtar. Korrektur eigenes Versehens in der Erstveröfftlichung," *ZNW* 69 (1978) 118-122.

1740 Kuhn, H. W. "Der Gekreuzigte von Giv'at ha-Mivtar. Bilanz einer Entdeckung," *Theologia Crucis, Signum Crucis*. Ed. C. Andresen and G. Klein (Fest. E. Dinkler). Tübingen: 1979, 303-334.

1741 Halperin, D. J. "Crucifixion, the Nahum Pesher, and the Rabbinic Penalty of Strangulation," *JJS* 32 (1981) 32-46.

1742 Kuhn, H. W. "Die Kreuzesstrafe während der frühen Kaiserzeit. Ihre Wirklichkeit und Wertung in der Umwelt des Urchristentums," *Aufstieg und Niedergang der römischen Welt*. 25.1. Berlin: 1982, 648-793.

1743 Harrison, S. J. "Cuero and 'crurifragium'," *Classical Quarterly* 33 (1983) 453-455.

1744 Tzaferis, V. "Crucifixion—The Archaeological Evidence," *BAR* 11 (1985) 44-53.

1745 Zias, J. and Sekeles, E. "The Crucified man from Giv'at ha-Mivtar: A Reappraisal," *IEJ* 35 (1985) 22-27.

XXIII. The Crucifixion of Jesus

Articles

1746 Milligan, W. "St. John's View of Jesus on the Cross," *Exp* 1st ser. 6 (1877) 17-36; 129-142.

1747 Conybeare, F. C. "New Testament Notes—(2) The Seamless Coat," *Exp* 4th ser. 9 (1894) 458-460.

1748 Ramsay, W. M. "The Sixth Hour," *Exp* 5th ser. 3 (1896) 457-459.

1749 Bacon, B. W. "Exegetical Notes: John 19:17-20," *BW* (1899) 423-425.

1750 Nestle, E. "The Seven Words from the Cross," *ExpT* 11 (1899-1900) 423-424.

1751 Nestle, E. "Luke xxiii.43," *ExpT* 11 (1899-1900) 429.

1752 Paton, W. R. "Die Kreuzigung Jesu," *ZNW* 2 (1901) 339-341.

1753 Nestle, E. "Der ungenähte Rock Jesu und der bunte Rock Josefs," *ZNW* 3 (1902) 169.

1754 Nestle, E. " 'Father, forgive them,' " *ExpT* 14 (1902-03) 285-286.

1755 White, J. D. W. "The Johannine View of the Crucifixion," *Exp* 6th ser. 7 (1903) 434-441.

1756 Davison, A. "The Crucifixion, Burial and Resurrection of Jesus," *Palestine Exploration Fund* 28 (1906) 124-129.

1757 Blathwayt, T. B. "The Penitent Thief," *ExpT* 18 (1906-07) 288.

1758 Lewis, A. S. "A New Reading of Luke xxiii.39," *ExpT* 18 (1906-07) 94-95.

1759 Martin, G. C. "A New Reading of Luke xxiii.39," *ExpT* 18 (1906-07) 334-335.

1760 Garvie, A. E. "The Desolation of the Cross," *Exp* 7th ser. 3 (1907) 507-527.

1761 Rudel, W. "Die letzten Worte Jesu," *NKZ* 21 (1910) 199-227.

1762 Rutherford, W. S. "The Seamless Coat," *ExpT* 22 (1910-11) 44-45.

1763 Kennedy, A. R. S. "The Soldiers' Portions (John xix.23,24)," *ExpT* 24 (1912-13) 90-91.

1764 Nestle, E. "Zum Ysop bei Johannes, Josephus und Philo," *ZNW* 14 (1913) 263-265.

1765 Moffatt, J. "Exegetica.—Luke xxiii.34," *Exp* 5th ser. 7 (1914) 92-93.

1766 Veale, H. C. " 'The Merciful Bystander,' " *ExpT* 28 (1916-17) 324-325.

1767 Saintyves, P. "Deux thèmes de la Passion et leur signification symbolique.—La tunique sans couture," *RArch* 17 (1917) 243-248.

1768 Henry, D. M. " 'Father, forgive them; for they know not what they do' (Luke xxiii.34)," *ExpT* 30 (1918-19) 87.

1769 Aytoun, R. A. "Himself he cannot save (Ps. xxii 29 and Mk. xv 31)," *JTS* 21 (1920) 245-248.

1770 Willcock, J. " 'When he had tasted' (Matt. xxvii.34)," *ExpT* 32 (1920-21) 426.

1771 Elliott, E. "When he had tasted (Matt. xxvii.34)," *ExpT* 33 (1921-22) 41-42.

1772 Kinsey, A. B. "Simon the Crucifier and Symeon the Prophet," *ExpT* 35 (1923-24) 84-88.

1773 Meyer, E. "Sinn und Tendenz der Schlusszene am Kreuz im Johannesevangelium (Joh. 19,25-27)," *Sitzungsberichte der Preussischen Akademie der Wissenschafter, phil. — hist. Klasse* (1924) 157-162.

1774 Young, T. E. "A Fresh Exposition of the Cries upon the Cross," *ExpT* 39 (1927-28) 93.

1775 Regard, P. F. "Le titre de la croix," *RArch* 28 (1928) 95-105.

1776 Dalman, G. "At the Cross," *Jesus-Jeshua*. Trans. P. R. Levertoff. London: 1929, 185-222.

1777 MacGregor, W. M. "The Words from the Cross. II. The Penitent Thief," *ExpT* 41 (1929-30) 151-154.

1778 Reid, J. "The Words from the Cross. I. 'Father, forgive them'," *ExpT* 41 (1929-30) 103-107.

1779 Simpson, H. L. "The Words from the Cross. V. 'I thirst'," *ExpT* 41 (1929-30) 103-107.

1780 Yates, T. "The Words from the Cross. VII," *ExpT* 41 (1929-30) 427-429.

1781 Bishop, E. F. F. "Simon and Lucius: Where did they come from?" *ExpT* 51 (1939-40) 148-153.

1782 Weisengoff, J. P. "Paradise and St. Luke 23:43," *AER* 103 (1940) 163-168.

1783 Holzmeister, U. "Die Finsternis beim Tode Jesu," *Bib* 22 (1941) 404-411.

1784 Evans, G. E. "The Sister of the Mother of Jesus," *RevExp* 44 (1947) 475-485.

1785 Davies, J. G. "Studies in Texts: The Cup of Wrath and the Cup of Blessing," *Theology* 51 (1948) 178-180.

1786 Dammers, A. H. "Studies in Texts, Luke xxiii,34a," *Theology* 52 (1949) 138-139.

1787 Grayston, K. "The Darkness of the Cosmic Sea: A Study of Symbolism in Mark's Narrative of the Crucifixion," *Theology* 55 (1952) 122-127.

1788 Daube, D. " 'For they know not what they do'," *StudiaPatristica* (TU 79 1961) 58-70.

1789 MacRae, G. W. "With me in Paradise," *Worship* 35 (1961) 235-240.

1790 Bishop, E. F. F. "Mary (of) Clopas and her Father," *ExpT* 73 (1961-62) 339.

1791 Taylor, V. "The Narrative of the Crucifixion," *NTS* 8 (1961-62) 333-334.

1792 Käser, W. "Exegetische und theologische Erwägungen zur Seligpreisung der Kinderlosen, Lc 23:29b," *ZNW* 54 (1963) 240-254.

1793 Wulf, F. " 'Jesus, gedenke meiner, wenn du in dein Königtum kommst' (Lk 23,42)," *GuL* 37 (1964) 1-3.

1794 Kingdon, H. P. "Messiaship and the Crucifixion," *SE* III (TU 88 1964) 67-86.

1795 Schwank, B. "Der erhöhte König: Jo 19,16b-22," *Sein und Sendung* 29 (1964) 244-254.

1796 Schwank, B. "Die ersten Gaben des erhöhten Königs (19,23-30)," *Sein und Sendung* 29 (1964), 292-309.

1797 Mahoney, A. "A New Look at 'The Third Hour' of Mk. 15:25," *CBQ* 28 (1966) 292-299.

1798 Spurrell, J. M. "An Interpretation of 'I Thirst,' " *CQR* 167 (1966) 12-18.

1799 Grelot, P. "Audjourd'hui tu seras avec moi dans le Paradis (Luc xxiii.43)," *RB* 74 (1967) 194-214.

1800 Trilling, W. "La promesse de Jésus au bon larron (Lc 23,33-43)," *AsSeign* 96 (1967) 31-39.

1801 Bammel, E. "Der Tod Jesu in einer 'Toledoth Jeschu' — Überlieferung," *ASTI* 6 (1968) 124-131. = *Judaica*. Tübingen: 1986, 1:196-204.

1802 Lee, G. M. "The Inscription on the Cross," *PEQ* 100 (1968) 144.

1803 Bampfylde, G. "John XIX 28, a Case for a Different Translation," *NovT* 11 (1969) 247-260.

1804 Trilling, W. "Der Tod Jesu, Ende der alten Weltzeit (Mk. 15.33-41)," *Christusverkündung in den synoptischen Evangelien*. Munich: 1969, 191-211.

1805 Aubineau, M. "La tunique sans couture du Christ. Exégèse patristique de Jean 19,13-24," *Kyriakon*. Ed. P. Granfield and J. A. Jungmann (Fest. J. Quasten). Münster: 1970, 100-127.

1806 Dvoracek, J. A. "Vom Leiden Gottes, Markus 15,29-34," *CV* 14 (1971) 231-252.

1807 Wansbrough, H. "The Crucifixion of Jesus," *Clergy Review* 56 (1971) 251-261.

1808 Smith, R. H. "Darkness at Noon: Mark's Passion Narrative," *CTM* 49 (1973) 325-338.

1809 Lee, G. M. "Mark 15,31: 'The Father of Alexander and Rufus,' " *NovT* 17 (1975) 303.

1810 Weeden, T. J. "The Cross as Power in Weakness (Mark 15:20b-41)," *The Passion in Mark: Studies on Mark 14-16*. Ed. W. H. Kelber. Philadelphia: 1976, 115-134.

1811 Crowe, J. "The *LAOS* at the Cross: Luke's Crucifixion Scene," *The Language of the Cross*. Ed. A. Lacomara. Chicago: 1979, 79-90.

1812 Flusser, D. "The Crucified One and the Jews," *Immanuel* 7 (1977) 25-37.

1813 Josuttis, M. "Die permanente Passion. Predigt über Markus 15, 33-39," *EvT* 38 (1978) 160-163.

1814 de la Potterie, I. "La tunique sans couture, symbole du Christ grand prêtre?" *Bib* 60 (1979) 255-269.

1815 Osborn, G. R. "Redactional Trajectories in the Crucifixion Narrative," *EvQ* 51 (1979) 80-96.

1816 de La Potterie, I. " 'Et à partir de cette heure, le Disciple l'acceueillit dans son intimité (Jn 19, 27b). Réflexions methodologiques sur l'interpretation d'un verset johannique," *Marianum* 42 (1980) 84-125.

1817 Buhlmann, W. "Die Kreuzigung Jesu," *Heiliges Land* 9 (1981) 3-12.

1818 Flusser, D. " 'Sie wissen nicht, was sie tun?' Geschichte eines Herrwortes," *Kontinuität und Einheit* (Fest. F. Mussner). Freiburg/Basel/Vienna: 1981, 393-410.

1819 Schreiber, J. "Die Bestattung Jesu. Redaktionsgeschichtliche Beobachtungen zu Mk 15,42-47 par.," *ZNW* 72 (1981) 142-177.

1820 Derrett, J. D. M. "The Two Malefactors (Lk xxiii. 33, 39-43)," *Studies in the New Testament*. Leiden: 1982, 3:200-214.

1821 Brower, K. "Elijah in the Markan Passion Narrative," *JSNT* 18 (1983) 85-101.

1822 Neyrey, J. H. "Jesus' Address to the Women of Jerusalem, (Lk. 23:27-31)—A Prophetic Judgment Oracle," *NTS* 29 (1983) 74-86.

1823 Bammel, E. "The *titulus*," *Jesus and the Politics of His Day*. Ed. E. Bammel and C. F. D. Moule. Cambridge: 1984, 353-364.

1824 de la Potterie, I. "La tunique 'non diviseé' de Jésus, symbole de l'unite messianique," *The New Testament Age*. Ed. W. C. Weinrich (Fest. B. Reicke). Macon: 1984, 1:127-138.

1825 Schwarz, G. "*HYSSŌPŌ PERITHENTES* (Johannes 19.29)," *NTS* 30 (1984) 625-626.

1826 Giblin, C. H. *The Destruction of Jerusalem according to Luke's Gospel: A Historical-Typological Moral*. AB 107. Rome: 1985, 93-104.

1827 Wilcox, M. "The Text of the Titulus in John 19.19-20 as Found in Some Italian Renaissance Paintings," *JSNT* 27 (1986) 113-116.

1828 Soards, M. L. "Tradition, Composition, and Theology in Jesus' Speech to the 'Daughters of Jerusalem' (Luke 23,26-32)," *Bib* 68 (1987) 221-244.

1829 Rodgers, P. "Mark 15:28," *EvQ* 61 (1989) 81-84.

See also 0252, 0257, 0290, 0297, 0295, 0297, 3011, 0315, 0348, 0353, 0369, 0372, 0374, 0375

XXIV. The Word
to the Mother of Jesus
and the Beloved Disciple

Book

1830 Serra, A. M. *Marie à Cana, Marie près de la croix (Jean 2,1-12 et 19,25-27)*. Paris: 1983.

Articles

1831 Kneller, C. A. "Joh. 19,26-27 bei den Kirchenvätern," *ZKT* 40 (1916) 597-612.

1832 Gaechter, P. "Die geistige Mutterschaft Marias. Ein Beitrag zur Erklärung von Jo. 19,26f.," *ZKT* 47 (1923) 391-429.

1833 Gossip, A. J. "The Words from the Cross. III. 'Woman, behold thy Son'," *ExpT* 41 (1929-30) 198-202.

1834 Unger, D. "A Note on John 19, 25-27," *CBQ* 9 (1947) 111-112.

1835 Preisker, H. "John 2,4 und 19,26," *ZNW* 42 (1949) 209-214.

1836 Bishop, E. F. F. "Mary (daughter of) Clopas (Jn, 19.25)," *ExpT* 65 (1953-54) 382-383.

1837 Boismard, M. E. "Note sur Jean 19,25-27," *RB* 61 (1954) 295-296.

1838 Thyes, A. "Jean 19,25-27 et la maternité spirituelle de Marie," *Marianum* 18 (1956) 80-117.

1839 Ceroke, C. P. "Mary's Maternal Role in John 19,25-27," *MarianStudies* 11 (1960) 123-151.

1840 Kerrigan, A. "Jn. 19,25-27 in the Light of Johannine Theology and the Old Testament," *Anton* 35 (1960) 369-416.

1841 Zerwick, M. "The Hour of the Mother—John 19:25-27," *TBT* 1 (1965) 1187-1194.

1842 Feuillet, A. "Les adieux du Christ à sa mère et la maternité spirituelle de Marie," *NRT* 86 (1964) 469-489. Eng. trans. (condensed) *TD* 15 (1967) 37-40.

1843 Feuillet, A. "L'heure de la femme (Jn. 16,21) et l'heure de la Mère de Jésus (Jn 19,25-27)," *Bib* 47 (1966) 169-184, 361-380, 557-573.

1844 Dauer, A. "Das Wort des Gekreuzigten an seine Mutter und den 'Jünger, den er liebte'—Eine traditionsgeschichtliche und theologische Untersuchung zu Joh 19,25-27," *BZ* 11 (1967) 222-239, 12 (1968) 80-93.

1845 Koehler, T. "Les principales interpretations traditionelles de Jn 19,25-27 pendant les douze premiers siècles," *Études Mariales* 26 (1968) 119-155.

1846 Langkammer, H. "Christ's 'Last Will and Testament' (John 19:26-27) in the Interpretation of the Fathers of the Church and the Scholastics," *Anton* 43 (1968) 99-109.

1847 Schürmann, H. "Jesu letzter Wille Joh. 19,26-27a," *Sapienter Ordinare.* (Fest E. Kleineidam). Leipzig: 1969, 105-123. = "Jesu Letzte Weisung: Joh. 19,26-27a," *Ursprung und Gestalt.* Düsseldorf: 1970, 13-28.

1848 de la Potterie, I. "Das Wort 'Siehe, deine Mutter' und die Annahme der Mutter durch den Jünger (Joh 19,27b)," *Neues Testament und Kirche.* Ed. J. Gnilka. (Fest. R. Schnackenburg). Freiburg: 1974, 191-219. = "La parole de Jésus 'Voici ta Mère' et l'accueil du Disciple (Jn 19,27b)," *Marianum* 36 (1974) 1-39.

1849 Brown, R. E. "The 'Mother of Jesus' in the Fourth Gospel," *L'Évangile de Jean. Sources, rédaction, théologie.* Ed. M. de Jonge. BETL 44. Gembloux: 1977, 307-310.

1850 Neirynck, F. *"EIS TA IDIA: Jn. 19,27 (et. 16,32),"* *ETL* 55 (1979) 357-365.

1851 Neirynck, F. "La traduction d'un verset johannique: Jn 19,27b," *ETL* 57 (1981) 83-106.

1852 Ben-Chorin, S. "A Jewish View of the Mother of Jesus," *Concilium* 168 (1983) 12-16.

1853 Chevallier, M. A. ''La fondation de 'l'Église' dans le quatrième évangile: Jn 19,25-30,'' *ETR* 58 (1983) 343-353.

XXV. The Cry of Dereliction

Books

1854 Hasenahl, W. *Die Gottverlassenheit des Christus nach dem Kreu-
zeswort bei Matthäus und Markus und das christologische Verständnis des griechisches Psalters. Eine exegetische Studie.* BFCT
39. Gütersloh, 1938.

1855 Rossé, G. *The Cry of Jesus on the Cross: A Biblical and Theological
Study.* Trans. S. W. Arndt. New York: 1988.

Articles

1856 Nestle, E. "Mark xv.34," *ExpT* 9 (1897-98) 521-522.

1857 Burkitt, F. C. "On St. Mark xv 34 in Cod. Bobbiensis," *JTS* 1 (1900)
278-279.

1858 Ballard, J. M. "The Fourth Cry from the Cross," *ExpT* 33 (1921-
22) 332-333.

1859 Gordon, T. C. "The Fourth Cry from the Cross," *ExpT* 34 (1922-
23) 380.

1860 Johnston, J. "The Words from the Cross IV. The Cry of Desolation," *ExpT* 41 (1929-30) 281-283.

1861 Sidersky, D. "La parole suprême de Jésus," *RHR* 103 (1931) 151-
154.

1862 Smith, F. "The Strangest 'Word' of Jesus," *ExpT* 44 (1932-33) 259-
261.

1863 Buckler, F. W. " 'Eli, Eli, Lama Sabacthani'?" *AJSL* 55 (1938) 378-
391.

1864 Lofthouse, W. F. "The Cry of Dereliction," *ExpT* 53 (1941-42) 188-192.

1865 Macleroy, C. M. "Notes on the Cry of Forsakenness on the Cross," *ExpT* 53 (1941-42) 326.

1866 Eichrodt, O. " 'Mein Gott' in Alten Testament," *ZAW* 61 (1945-46) 3-16.

1867 Kenneally, W. J. "Eli, Eli, Lamma Sabacthani? (Mt. 27:46)," *CBQ* 8 (1946) 124-134.

1868 Zimmermann, F. "The Last Words of Jesus," *JBL* 66 (1947) 465-466.

1869 Guillaume, A. "Mt. 27,46 in the Light of the Dead Sea Scroll of Isaiah," *PEQ* 83 (1951) 78-81.

1870 Sahlin, H. "Zum Verständnis von drei Stellen des Markus-Evangeliums (Mc 4,26-29; 7,18f; 15,34)," *Bib* 33 (1952) 53-66.

1871 Worden, T. " 'My God, my God, why hast Thou forsaken me?' " *Scr* 6 (1953) 9-16.

1872 Blight, W. "The Cry of Dereliction," *ExpT* 68 (1956-57) 285.

1873 Read, D. H. C. "Expository Problems: The Cry of Dereliction," *ExpT* 68 (1956-57) 260-262.

1874 Rehm, M. "Eli, Eli, lamma sabacthani," *BZ* 2 (1958) 275-278.

1875 Baker, N. B. "The Cry of Dereliction," *ExpT* 10 (1958-59) 54-55.

1876 Gnilka, J. "Mein Gott, mein Gott, warum hast du mich verlassen," (Mk 15,34 Par.), *BZ* 3 (1959) 294-297.

1877 Bligh, J. "Christ's Death Cry," *HeyJ* 1 (1960) 142-146.

1878 Boman, T. "Das letzte Wort Jesu," *ST* 17 (1963) 103-119.

1879 Lacan, M. F. "Mon Dieu, Mon Dieu, pourquoi? Mt. 27,46," *LumVit* 66 (1964) 33-54.

1880 Floris, E. "L'abandon de Jésus et la mort de Dieu," *ETR* 42 (1967) 277-298.

1881 Gese, H. "Psalm 22 und das Neue Testament," *ZTK* 65 (1968) 1-22.

1882 Danker, F. W. "The Demonic Secret in Mark: A Reexamination of the Cry of Dereliction (15:34), *ZNW* 61 (1970) 48-69.

1883 Holst, T. "The Cry of Dereliction—Another Point of View," *Springfielder* 35 (1972) 286-289.

1884 Lange, H. D. "The Relationship Between Psalm 22 and the Passion Narrative," *CTM* 48 (1972) 610-621.

1885 Bobichon, M. "Eli Eli lema sebachtani!" *BTS* 149 (1973) 4-6.

1886 Braumann, G. "Wozu (Mark 15,34)," *Theokratia*. Leiden: 1973, 2:155-165.

1887 Basset, J. C. "Le psaume 22 (LXX: 21) et la croix chez les péres," *RPR* 54 (1974) 383-389.

1888 Reumann, J. H. "Psalm 22 at the Cross. Lament and Thanksgiving for Jesus Christ," *Int* 28 (1974) 39-58.

1889 Schützeichel, H. "Der Todesschrei Jesus—Bemerkungen zu einer Theologie des Kreuzes," *TrierTZ* 83 (1974) 1-16.

1890 Senior, D. P. "A Death Song," *TBT* (1974) 1457-1463.

1891 Trudinger, L. P. " 'Eli, Eli, Lama Sabachthani': A Cry of Dereliction or Victory?" *JETS* 19 (1974) 235-238.

1892 Rogers, P. "The Death of Jesus in the Gospel of Mark," *The Language of the Cross*. Ed. A. Lacomara. Chicago: 1977, 53-74.

1893 Stuhlmueller, C. "Faith and Abandonment in the Psalms of Supplication," *The Language of the Cross*. Ed. A. Lacomara. Chicago: 1977, 1-28.

1894 Léon-Dufour, X. "Le dernier cri de Jésus," *Études* 348 (1978) 666-682.

1895 Deissler, A. " 'Mein Gott, warum hast du mich verlassen …!' (Ps 22,2): Das Reden zu Gott und von Gott in den Psalmen—am Beispiel von Psalm 22," *"Ich will euer Gott werden": Beispiele biblischen Redens vor Gott*. Ed. H. Merklein und E. Zenger. SBS 100. Stuttgart: 1981, 97-121.

1896 Cohn-Sherbok, D. "Jesus' Cry on the Cross: An Alternative View," *ExpT*, 93 (1981-82) 215-217.

1897 Sagne, J. C. "The Cry of Jesus on the Cross," *Concilium* 169 (1983) 52-58.

1898 Burchard, C. "Markus 15,34," *ZNW* 74 (1983) 1-11.

1899 Caza, L. "Le relief que Marc a donné au cri de la croix," *ScEs* 39 (1987) 171-191.

1900 Guichard, D. "La reprise du Psaume 22 dans le récit de la mort de Jésus," *Foi et Vie* 87 (1988) 59-65.

See also 0064, 0197, 0283, 0302, 0322, 0338, 0867, 1760

XXVI. The Death of Jesus

Books

1901 Stoeffe, O. *Physiologie Unmöglichkeit des Todes Christi am Kreuze.* Bonn: 1912.

1902 Stroud, W. *Treatise on the Physical Cause of the Death of Christ and its Relation to the Practice of Christianity.* 2d ed. London: 1971.

1903 Gilly, R. *Passion de Jésus. Les conclusions d'un médecin.* Paris: Fayard: 1985.

Articles

1904 Goodwin, D. R. "*Theou huios* Matt. xxvii.54, and Mark xv.39," *JBL* 6 (1886) 129-131.

1905 Brown, D. "The Veil of the Temple Rent in Twain from the Top to the Bottom," *Exp* 5th ser. 2 (1895) 158-160.

1906 Dechent, H. "Zur Auslegung der Stelle Joh. 19,35," *TSK* 72 (1899) 446-467.

1907 Blass, F. "Über Ev. Joh. 19,35," *TSK* 75 (1902) 128-133.

1908 Nestle, E. "Die Sonnenfinsternis bei Jesu Tod," *ZNW* 3 (1902) 246-247.

1909 Mann, C. "The Centurion at the Cross," *ExpT* 20 (1908-09) 563-564.

1910 Simpson, A. R. "The Broken Heart of Jesus," *Exp* 8th ser. 2 (1911) 310-321.

1911 Nestle, E. "John xix.37," *ExpT* 24 (1912-13) 92.

1912 Vogels, H. J. "Der Lanzenstich vor dem Tode Jesu," *BZ* 10 (1912) 396-405.

1913 Haensler, B. "Zu Jo. 19,35," *BZ* 11 (1913) 44-48.

1914 Clarke, W. K. L. "St. Luke and the Pseudepigrapha: Two Parallels," *JTS* 15 (1913-14) 597-599.

1915 vom Kasten, J. "Der Lanzenstich bei Mt 27,49," *BZ* 12 (1914) 32-34.

1916 Vogels, H. J. "Der Lanzenstich vor dem Tode Jesu," *BZ* 12 (1914) 396-405.

1917 Kraft, B. "Das Koptische Irenaeus-Fragment De Lagardes zu Jo. 19,34," *BZ* 13 (1915) 354-355.

1918 Harris, J. R. "The Origin of a Famous Lucan Gloss," *ExpT* 35 (1923-24) 7-10.

1919 Chase, F. H. "Two Notes on St. John's Gospel (John. 19,35; 8,56)," *JTS* 26 (1924-25) 381.

1920 Simpson, J. G. "The Words from the Cross. VI. 'It is finished'," *ExpT* 41 (1929-30) 343-347.

1921 Barton, G. A. " 'A Bone of Him Shall Not be Broken': John 19:36," *JBL* 49 (1930) 13-19.

1922 d'Ales, A. "La condition du corps du Christ dans la mort," *RSR* 11 (1931) 200-201.

1923 Schneider, C. "Der Hauptmann am Kreuz," *ZNW* 33 (1934) 1-17.

1924 Killermann, S. "Die Finsternis beim Tode Jesu," *TGl* 33 (1941) 165-166.

1925 Kilpatrick, G. D. "A Theme of the Lucan Passion Story and Luke XXIII.48," *JTS* 43 (1942) 34-36.

1926 O'Rahilly, A. "The Title of the Cross," *Irish Ecclesiatical Record* 65 (1945) 289-297.

1927 Williams, W. H. "The Veil was Rent," *RevExp* 48 (1951) 275-285.

1928 Sahlin, H. "Zum Verständnis von drei Stellen des Mk-Ev," *Bib* 33 (1952) 62-66.

1929 Daube, D. "The Veil of the Temple," *The New Testament and Rabbinic Judaism. London: 1956*, 23-26.

1930 Bratcher, R. G. "A Note on *huios theou* (Mark XV.39)," *ExpT* 68 (1956-57) 27-28.

1931 Leenhardt, F. J. "Réflexions sur la mort de Jésus-Christ," *RHPR* 37 (1957) 18-23.

1932 Sons, E. "Zur Todesursache bei der Kreuzigung," *Benediktinische Monatschrift* 33 (1957) 101-106.

1933 Pelletier, A. "La tradition synoptique du 'voile dechiré' à la lumière des realités archéologiques," *RSR* 46 (1958) 161-180.

1934 Schwank, B. " 'Sie werden schauen auf ihn, den sie durchbohrt haben' (19:31-42)," *Sein und Sendung* 29 (1964) 340-353.

1935 Grassi, J. A. "Ezekiel xxxvii. 1-14 and the New Testament," *NTS* 11 (1964-65) 162-164.

1936 Driver, G. R. "Two Problems in the New Testament," *JTS* 16 (1965) 327-337.

1937 Brehant, J. "What was the Medical Cause of Christ's Death?" *Medical World News* (Oct. 27, 1966) 154-159.

1938 Abramowski, L. and Goodman, A. E. "Luke xxiii.46 *paratithemai* in a Rare Syriac Rendering," *NTS* 13 (1966-67) 290-291.

1939 Lindeskog, G. "The Veil of the Temple," *ConNT* XI (1947) 132-137.

1940 Michaels, J. R. "The Centurion's Confession and the Spear Thrust," *CBQ* 29 (1967) 102-109.

1941 Johnson, S. L., Jr. "The Death of Christ (Mt. 27:45-46)," *BSac* 125 (1968) 10-19.

1942 Bligh, P. H. "A Note on *Huios Theou* in Mark 15,39," *ExpT* 80 (1968-69) 51-53.

1943 Bampfylde, G. "John xix 28, a Case for a Different Translation," *NovT* 11 (1969) 247-260.

1944 Trilling, W. "Der Tod Jesu, Ende der alten Weltzeit (Mk 15,33-41)," *Christusverkündigung in den synoptischen Evangelien*. Munich: 1969, 191-211.

1945 Guy, H. A. "Son of God in Mk. 15,39," *ExpT* 81 (1970) 151.

1946 Pobee, J. "The Cry of the Centurion — A Cry of Defeat," *The Trial of Jesus*. Ed. E. Bammel. SBT 2d. ser. 13. Naperville, IL.: 1970, 91-102.

1947 Ball, R. O. "Physical Cause of the Death of Jesus. A Theological Comment," *ExpT* 83 (1971-72) 248.

1948 Bucher, G. "Elements for an Analysis of the Gospel Text: The Death of Jesus," *Modern Language Notes* 86 (1971) 835-844.

1949 Leese, K. "Physical Cause of the Death of Jesus: 2) A Medical Opinion," *ExpT* 83 (1972) 248.

1950 Sawyer, J. F. A. "Why is a Solar Eclipse Mentioned in the Passion Narrative (Luke XXIII.44-5)?" *JTS* 23 (1972) 124-128.

1951 Wilkinson, J. "The Physical Cause of the Death of Christ," *ExpT* 83 (1972) 104-107.

1952 Crossan, J. D. "Mark and the Relatives of Jesus," *NovT* 15 (1973) 81-113.

1953 Harner, P. B. "Qualitative Anarthrous Predicate Nouns: Mark 15,39 and John 1,1," *JBL* (1973) 75-87.

1954 Kempthorne, R. " 'As God is my Witness!' " John 19,34-35," *SE* VI (TU 112, 1973) 287-290.

1955 Trilling, W. "Le Christ, roi crucifié, Lc 23,35-43," *AsSeign* 65 (1973) 56-65.

1956 Lamarche, P. "La mort du Christ et le voile du temple selon Marc," *NRT* 96 (1974) 583-599.

1957 Lange, J. "Zur Ausgestaltung der Szene vom Sterben Jesu in den synoptischen Evangelien," *Biblische Randbemerkungen*. Ed. H. Merklein and J. Lange (Fest. R. Schackenburg). Freiburg: 1974, 40-55.

1958 Schützeichel, H. "Der Todesschrei Jesu — Bemerkungen zu einer Theologie des Kreuzes," *TTZ* 83 (1974) 1-16.

1959 Faessler, M. "Marc 15,21-39: La mort de Jésus," *Bulletin du Centre Protestant d' Études* 28 (1976) 28-30.

1960 Lee, G. M. "Two Notes on St. Mark," *NovT* 18 (1976) 36.

1961 Vouga, F. "Marc 15,21-39: La mort de Jésus," *Bulletin du Centre Protestant d' Études* 28 (1976) 25-28.

1962 Seynaeve, J. "Les citations scripturaires en Jn 19,36-37: Une preuve en faveur de la typologie de l'Agneau Pascal?" *Revue Africaine de Theologie* 1 (1977) 67-76.

1963 Léon-Dufour, X. "Der Todesschrei Jesu," *Theologie der Gegen-wart* 21 (1978) 172-178.

1964 Stock, K. "Das Bekenntnis des Centurio, Mk. 15,39 im Rahmen des Markusevangeliums," *ZKT* 100 (1978) 289-301.

1965 Aguirre, R. "Cross and Kingdom in Matthew's Theology," *TD* 29 (1981) 149-153.

1966 Leroy, H. " 'Kein Bein wird ihm zerbrochen werden' (Jo 19,31-37). Zur johanneischen Interpretation des Kreuzes," *Eschatologie. Bibeltheologische und philosophische Studien zum Verhältnis von Erlösungswelt und Wirklichkeitbeältigung* Ed. R. Kilian, K. Funk and P. Fassi (Fest. E Neuhausler). St. Ottilien: 1981, 73-81.

1967 Chronis, H. L. "The Torn Veil: Cultus and Christology in Mark 15,37-39," *JBL* 101 (1982) 97-114.

1968 Riebl, M. "Jesu Tod und Auferstehung—Hoffnung für unser Sterben. Beispiel didaktisch aufbreiteter neuerer Bibelauslegung," *BLit* 57 (1984) 208-213.

1969 de Jonge, M. "Two Interesting Interpretations of the Rending of the Temple-veil in the Testaments of the Twelve Patriarchs," *Bijdragen* 46 (1985) 350-362.

1970 Manus, C. U. "The Centurion's Confession of Faith (Mk 15:39): Its Reflections on Mark's Christology and Its Significance in the Life of African Christians," *BTA* 7 (1985) 261-278.

1971 Edwards, W. D., Gabel, W. J. and Hosmer, F. E. "On the Physical Death of Christ," *JAMA* 255 (1986) 1455-1463.

1972 Karris, R. J. "Luke 23:47 and the Lucan View of Jesus' Death," *JBL* 105 (1986) 65-74.

1973 Sylva, D. "The Temple Curtain and Jesus' Death in the Gospel of Luke," *JBL* 105 (1986) 239-250.

1974 Jackson, H. M. "The Death of Jesus in Mark and the Miracle of the Cross," *NTS* 33 (1987) 16-37.

1975 Johnson, E. S. "Is Mark 15:39 the Key to Mark's Christology?" *JSNT* 31 (1987) 3-22.

1976 Motyer, S. "The Rending of the Veil: A Markan Pentecost?" *NTS* 33 (1987) 155-157.

1977 Edwards, W. D., Gabel, W. J. , and Hosmer, F. E. "On the Physical Death of Jesus Christ," *JAMA* 255 (1986) 1455-1463.

1978 Smith, D. E. "An Autopsy of an Autopsy: Biblical Illiteracy Among Medical Doctors," *Westar Magazine* 1 (1987) 3-6, 14-15.

1979 Bergmeier, R. "*TETELESTAI* Joh 19:30," *ZNW* 79 (1988) 282-290.

1980 Zugibe, F. T. "Two Questions About Crucifixion: Does the Victim Die of Asphyxiation? Would Nails in the Hands Hold the Weight of the Body?" *Bible Review* 5 (1989) 34-43.

See also 0221, 0295, 0297, 0310, 0311, 0315, 0328, 0334, 0335, 0338, 0387, 0390

XXVII. The Blood
and the Water
From the Side of Christ

Books

1981 Hultkvist, G. *What Does the Expression ''Blood and Water'' Mean in the Gospel of John 19,34? Vrigstad, Sweden: 1947.*

1982 Maguire, A. A. *Blood and Water. The Wounded Side of Christ in Early Christian Literature.* SST 108. Washington: 1958.

1983 Poncelet, M. *Les Mystère du sang et de l'eau dans l'évangile de saint Jean.* Paris: 1961.

Articles

1984 Lossen, W. ''Blut und Wasser aus der Seite Jesu,'' *TGl* 33 (1941) 48-59.

1985 Braun, F. M. ''L'eau et l'Esprit,'' *RevThom* 49 (1949) 5-30.

1986 Sava, A. F. ''The Wounds of Christ,'' *CBQ* 16 (1954) 438-443.

1987 Sava, A. F. ''The Wound in the Side of Christ,'' *CBQ* 19 (1957) 343-346.

1988 Sava, A. F. ''The Blood and Water from the Side of Christ,'' *AER* 138 (1958) 341-345.

1989 Lefevre, A. ''Die Seitenwunde Jesu,'' *GuL* 33 (1960) 86-96.

1990 Winandy, J. ''Le témoignage du sang et de l'eau (Jean 19,17-37),'' *BVC* 31 (1960) 19-27.

1991 Ford, J. M. " 'Mingled Blood' from the Side of Christ (John xix.34)," *NTS* 15 (1968-69) 337-338.

1992 Wilkinson, J. "The Incident of the Blood and Water in John 19:34," *SJT* 28 (1975) 149-178.

1993 Dunlop, L. "The Pierced Side. Focal Point of Johannine Theology," *TBT* 86 (1976) 960-965.

1994 Venetz, H. J. "Zeuge des Erhöhten. Ein exegetischer Beitrag zu Joh 19,31-37," *FZPT* 23 (1976) 81-111.

1995 Richter, G. "Blut und Wasser aus der durchbohrten Seite Jesu (Joh. 19,34b)," *MTZ* 21 (1970) 1-21. = *Studien zum Johannesevangelium*. BU 13. Ed. J. Hainz. Regensburg: 1977, 120-142.

1996 Vellanickal, M. "Blood and Water," *Jeevadhara* 8 (1978) 218-230.

1997 Heer, J. "Das johanneische Bild des Durchbohrten in seiner soteriologischen Bedeutung," *Christusglaube und Christusverehrung*. Ed. L. Scheffczyk. Aschaffenburg: 1982, 37-54.

1998 Pennells, S. "The Spear Thrust (Mt 27.49b, v.l./Jn 19.34)," *JSNT* 19 (1983) 99-115.

1999 de la Potterie, I. "Le symbolisme du sang et de l'eau en Jn 19,34," *Didaskalia* 14 (1984) 201-230.

2000 Vandana, S. "Wasser des Heils. Eine indische Deutung der durchbohrten Seite Jesu (Joh 19,31-37)," *Wir werden bei ihm wohnen. Das Johannesevangelium in indischer Deutung*. Theologie der Dritten Welt 6. Freiburg/Basel/Vienna: 1984, 157-172.

2001 Grassi, J. A. "Eating Jesus' Flesh and Drinking his Blood: The Centrality and Meaning of John 6:51-58," *BTB* 17 (1987) 24-30.

2002 Brock, S. P. " 'One of the Soldiers Pierced': The Mysteries hidden in the Side of Christ," *Christian Orient* 9 (1988) 49-59.

XXVIII. The Resurrection of the Saints

Book

2003 Fascher, E. *Das Weib des Pilatus (Matthäus 27,19). Die Auferer-weckung der Heiligen (Matthäus 27, 51-53). Zwei Studien zur Geschichte der Schriftauslegung.* Halle: 1951.

Articles

2004 Nestle, E. "Matth. 27,51 und Parallelen," *ZNW* 3 (1902) 167-168.

2005 Blinzler, J. "Zur Erklärung von Mt. 27.51b-53. Totenauferstehung am Karfreitag?" *TGl* 35 (1943) 91-93.

2006 Fuller, R. C. "The Bodies of the Saints, Matt. 27,52-53," *Scr* 3 (1948) 86-88.

2007 Zeller, H. "Corpora Sanctorum. Eine Studie zu Mt. 27,52-53," *ZKT* 71 (1949) 385-465.

2008 Winklhofer, A. "Corpora Sanctorum (Mt 27,51ff). Zu H. Zellers gleichnämigen Beitrag in *Ztschr f. k. Theologie* 71 (1949)," *TQ* 133 (1953) 30-67, 210-217.

2009 Essame, W. G. "Matthew xxvii 51-54 and John v 25-29," *ExpT* 76 (1964-65) 103.

2010 Senior, D. P. "The Death of God's Son and the Beginning of the New Age (Matthew 27:51-54)," *The Language of the Cross*. Ed. A. Lacomara. Chicago: 1977.

2011 Wenham, J. W. "When Were the Saints Raised? A Note on the Punctuation of Matthew xxvii 51-53," *JTS* 32 (1981) 150-152.

2012 de Jonge, M. "Matthew 27:51 in Early Christian Exegesis," Ed. G. W. E. Nickelsburg and G. W. MacRae. (Fest. N. Dahl) Philadelphia: 1986, 67-79.

2013 Maisch, I. "Die Österliche Dimension des Todes Jesu. Zur Österverkündigung im Mt 27,51-54," *Auferstehung Jesu— Auferstehung der Christen. Deutungen des Österglaubens.* Ed. I Broer (Fest. A. Vögtle). QD 105. Freiburg/Basel/Vienna: 1986, 96-123.

2014 Witherup, R. D. "The Death of Jesus and the Raising of the Saints: Matthew 27:51-54 in Context," *SBLASP* 1987 574-585.

See also 0236, 0252, 0257, 0258

XXIX. The Burial of Jesus

Books

2015 Klein, S. *Tod und Begräbnis in Palästina zur Zeit der Tannaiten.* Berlin: 1908.

2016 Baldensperger, G. *Le Tombeau Vide.* Paris: 1935.

2017 Braun, F. M. *Le Sépulture de Jésus.* Paris: 1937.

2018 Broer, I. *Die Urgemeinde und das Grab Jesu. Eine Analyse der Grablegungsgeschichte im Neuen Testament.* SANT 31. Munich: 1972.

Articles

2019 Bender, A. P. "Beliefs and Rites and Customs of the Jews Concerning Death, Burial and Mourning," *JQR* 6 (1894) 317-347; 664-671; 7 (1894-95) 101-118; 259-269.

2020 von Dobschütz, E. "Joseph von Arimathia," *ZKG* 23 (1902) 1-17.

2021 Buchler, A. "L'enterrement des criminels d'après le Talmud et le Midrash," *REJ* 46 (1903) 74-88.

2022 Vincent, L. H. "Garden Tomb: historie d'un mythe," *RB* 34 (1925) 401-431.

2023 Bornhäuser, K. "Die Kreuzesabnahme und das Begräbnis Jesu," *NKZ* 42 (1931) 38-56.

2024 Holtzmann, O. "Das Begräbnis Jesu," *ZNW* 30 (1931) 311-313.

2025 Burkitt, F. C. "A Note on Lk. xxiii 51 in the Dura Fragment," *JTS* 36 (1935) 258-259.

2026 Braun, F. M. "La sépulture de Jésus," *RB* 45 (1936) 34-52; 184-200; 346-363. = *La sépulture de Jésus à propos de trois livres recents*. Paris: 1937.

2027 Joüon, P. "Matthieu xxvii,59: *sindon kathara*," *RSR* 24 (1934) 93-95.

2028 Dalman, G. "Golgotha and the Sepulchre," *Sacred Sites and Ways*. New York: 1935, 346-381.

2029 Jackson, C. "Joseph of Arimathea," *JR* 16 (1936) 332-340.

2030 Hynek, R. W. "Das Grabtuch Christi," *Klerusblatt* 22 (1941) 289-291.

2031 O'Rahilly, A. "The Burial of Christ," *Irish Ecclesiastical Record* 58 (1941) 302-316; 439-503; 59 (1942) 150-171.

2032 Masson, C. "L'ensevelissement de Jésus (Marc xv,42-47)," *RTP* 31 (1943) 192-203.

2033 Blinzler, J. "Zur Auslegung der Evangelienberichte über Jesu Begräbnis," *MTZ* 3 (1952) 403-414.

2034 Bulst, W. "Untersuchungen zum Begräbnis Christi," *MTZ* 3 (1952) 244-255.

2035 Gaechter, P. "Zum Begräbnis Jesu," *ZKT* 75 (1953) 220-225.

2036 Wocken, A. "Der Reiche im AT. Ein Beitrag zu Jes 53,9," *TTZ* 62 (1953) 52-58.

2037 Kennard, S. "The Burial of Jesus," *JBL* 74 (1955) 227-238.

2038 Dhanis, E. "L'ensevelissement de Jésus et la visite au tombeau dans l'évangile de saint Marc (xv,40-xvi,8)," *Greg* 39 (1958) 367-410.

2039 Mercurio, R. "A Baptismal Motif in the Gospel Narratives of the Burial, " *CBQ* 21 (1959) 39-54.

2040 Michel, O. "Jüdische Bestattung und urchristliche Ostergeschichte," *Jud* 16 (1960) 1-5.

2041 Masson, C. "L'ensevelissement de Jésus (Marc 15:42-47)," *Vers les sources d'eau vive*. Lausanne: 1961, 102-113.

2042 Smith, K. "The Guard on the Tomb," *HeyJ* 2 (1961) 157-159.

2043 Smith, R. H. "The Tomb of Jesus," *BA* 30 (1967) 74-90.

2044 Lee, G. M. "The Guard at the Tomb," *Theology* 72 (1969) 169-175.

2045 Lee, G. M. "What Happened to the Body of Jesus?" *ExpT* 81 (1969-70) 307-310.

2046 Whitaker, D. "What Happened to the Body of Jesus?" *ExpT* 81 (1969-70) 307-310.

2047 Hemelsoet, B. "L'ensevelissement selon saint Jean," *Studies in John*. NovTSup 24 (Fest. J. N. Sevenster). Leiden: 1970, 47-65.

2048 Briend, J. "La sépulture d'un crucifié," *BTS* 133 (1971) 6-10.

2049 Curtis, K. P. G. "Three Points of Contact between Matthew and John in the Burial and Resurrection Narratives," *JTS* 23 (1972) 440-444.

2050 Crossan, J. D. "Mark and the Relatives of Jesus," *NovT* 15 (1973) 81-113.

2051 Blinzler, J. "Die Grablegung Jesu in historischer Sicht," *Resurrexit. Actes du symposium international sur la Résurrection de Jésus*. Ed. E. Dhanis. Rome: 1974, 56-107.

2052 Giblin, C. H. "Structural and Thematic Correlations in the Matthaean Burial-Resurrection Narrative (Matt. xxviii, 57-xxviii,20)," *NTS* 21 (1974-75) 406-420.

2053 Barrick, W. D. "The Rich Man from Arimathea (Matt. 27:57-60), and 1Q Isaa," *JBL* (1977) 235-239.

2054 Schreiber, J. "Die Bestattung Jesu. Redaktionsgeschichtliche Beobachtungen zu Mk 15:42-47 par.," *ZNW,* 72 (1981) 141-177.

2055 Liebowitz, H. "Jewish Burial Practices in the Roman Period," *The Mankind Quarterly* 22 (1981-82) 107-117.

2056 de Kruijf, T. C. " 'More than Half a hundredweight' of Spices (John 19,39 *NEB*). Abundance and Symbolism in the Gospel of John," *Bijdragen* 43 (1982) 234-239.

2057 Hachlili, R. and Killebrew, A. "Jewish Funerary Customs During the Second Temple Period, in the Light of the Excavations at the Jericho Necropolis," *PEQ* 115 (1983) 115-126.

2058 Craig, W. L. "The Guard at the Tomb," *NTS* 30 (1984) 273-281.

2059 Figueras, P. "Jewish Ossuaries and Secondary Burial: Their Significance for Early Christianity," *Immanuel* 19 (1984-85) 41-57.

2060 Riesner, R. "Golgota und die Archaeologie," *BK* 40 (1985) 21-26.

2061 Bahat, D. "Does the Holy Sepulchre Church Mark the Burial of Jesus?" *BAR* 12 (1986) 26-45.

2062 Barkay, G. "The Garden Tomb—Was Jesus Buried Here?" *BAR* 12 (1986) 40-57.

2063 Brown, R. E. "The Burial of Jesus (Mark 15:42-47)," *CBQ* 50 (1988) 233-245.

2064 Sylva, D. D. "Nicodemus and his Spices (John 19:39)," *NTS* 34 (1988) 148-151.

See also 0200, 0328, 0605, 1819, 2109

XXX. The Shroud of Turin

Books

2065 Vignon, P. *Le Saint Suaire de Turin devant la science, l'archáeo-logie, l'histoire, l'iconographie, la logique.* 2 ed. Paris: 1939.

2066 Blinzler, J. *Das Turinner Grablinnen und die Wissenschaft.* Ettal: 1952.

2067 Rinaldi, P. M. *The Man in the Shroud.* London: 1974.

2068 Hoare, R. *The Testimony of the Shroud.* London: 1978.

2069 Sox, H. D. *File on the Shroud.* London: 1978.

2070 Wilson, I. *The Shroud of Turin.* Garden City, NY: 1978.

2071 Sox, H. D. *The Image on the Shroud: Is the Turin Shroud a Forgery?* London: 1981.

2072 Stevenson, K. E. and Habermas, G. R.. *Verdict on the Shroud.* Ann Arbor: 1981.

2073 Zugibe, F. T. *The Cross and the Shroud.* Garnerville, NY: 1981.

2074 Heller, J. H. *Report on the Shroud of Turin.* Briarcliff Manor, NY: 1983.

2075 Nickell, J. *Inquest on the Shroud of Turin.* Buffalo: 1983.

2076 Rinaldi, P. M. *I Saw the Holy Shroud of Christ.* New Rochelle, NY: 1983.

2077 Tribbe, F. C. *Portrait of Jesus? The Illustrated Story of the Shroud of Turin.* New York: 1983.

2078 Drews, R. *In Search of the Shroud of Turin. New Light on Its History and Origins.* Totowa, NJ: 1984.

2079 Hoare, R. *A Piece of the Cloth.* Wellingborough: 1984.

2080 Walter, J. J. *Le visage du Christ.* 1984.

2081 Maher, R. W. *Science, History and the Shroud of Turin*. New York: 1985.

2082 Thomas, J. C. *"C'est le Seigneur.* 1985.

2083 O'Rahilly, A. *The Crucified*. Ed. J. A. Gaughan. Dublin: 1985.

2084 Dubarle, A. M. *Histoire ancienne du linceul de Turin jusq'au XIIIe siecle*. Paris: 1986.

2085 Wilson, I. *The Mysterious Shroud*. Garden City, NY: 1986.

2086 Bulst, W. and Pfeiffer, H. *Das Turiner Grabtuch und das Christen-bild. Band I: Das Grabtuch. Forschungsberichte und Untersuch-ungen*. Frankfurt am Main: 1987.

Articles

2087 Wuenschel, E. A. "The Holy Shroud of Turin: Eloquent Record of the Passion," *AER* 93 (1935) 441-472.

2088 Braun, F. M. "Le Linceul de Turin et l'Évangile de Saint Jean," *NRT* 66 (1939) 900-935, 1025-1046.

2089 Braun, F. M. "Le Linceul de Turin. Note complementaire," *NRT* 67 (1940) 322-324.

2090 O'Gorman, P. W. "The Holy Shroud of Jesus Christ: The New Dis-covery of the Cause of the Impression," *AER* 102 (1940) 208-226.

2091 Wuenschel, E. A. "The Holy Shroud: Present State of the Ques-tion," *AER* 102 (1940) 465-486.

2092 Wuenschel, E. A. "The Shroud of Turin and the Burial of Christ," *CBQ* 7 (1945) 405-437.

2093 McNaspy, C. J. "The Shroud of Turin," *CBQ* 7 (1945) 144-164.

2094 Wuenschel, E. A. "The Truth About the Holy Shroud," *AER* 129 (1953) 3-19; 100-114; 170-187.

2095 Robinson, J. A. T. "Re-investigating the Shroud of Turin," *The-ology* 80 (1977) 194-197.

2096 Culliton, B. J. "Science Investigates the Shroud of Turin," *Science* 201 (1978) 235.

2097 Sox, H. D. "The Authenticity of the Shroud," *ClerRev* 43 (1978) 250-256.

2098 Nickell, J. "The Turin Shroud: Fake? Fact? Photograph?" *Popular Photography* 85 (1979) 97-99, 146-147.

2099 Bortin, V. "Science and the Shroud of Turin," *BA* 43 (1980) 109-117.

2100 Accetta, J. S. and Baumgart, J. S. "Infrared Reflectance Spectroscopy and Thermographic Investigations of the Shroud of Turin," *Applied Optics* 19 (June 15, 1980) 1921-1929.

2101 Cohn-Sherbok, D. "The Jewish Shroud of Turin?" *ExpT* 92 (1980) 13-16.

2102 Gilbert, R. and Gilbert, M. "Ultraviolet-visible Reflectance and Fluorescence Spectra of the Shroud of Turin," *Applied Optics* 19 (June 15, 1980) 1930-1946.

2103 Heller, J. H. and Adler, A. D. "Blood on the Shroud of Turin," *Applied Optics* 19 (Aug. 15, 1980) 2742-2744.

2104 Morris, R. A.; Schwalbe, L. A.; and London, J. R. "X-Ray Fluorescence Investigation of the Shroud of Turin," *X-Ray Spectrometry* 9 (1980) 40-47.

2105 Burden, A. "Shroud of Mystery," *Science* 81 (1981) 76-83.

2106 Pellicori, S. and Evans, M. "The Shroud of Turin through the Microscope," *Archaeology* 34/1 (1981) 35-43.

2107 Feuillet, A. The Identification and Disposition of the Funerary Linens of Jesus' Burial According to the Data of the fourth Gospel," *Shroud Spectrum International* 1 (1982) 13-23.

2108 Jennings, J. A. "Putting the Shroud to Rest," *The Christian Century* 100 (1983) 552-554.

2109 Smith, D. M. "Mark 15:46: The Shroud of Turin as a Problem of History and Faith," *BA* 46 (1983) 251-254.

2110 Shorter, M. "The Sign of the Linen Cloths: The Fourth Gospel and the Holy Shroud of Turin," *JSNT* 17 (1983) 90-96.

2111 Brown, R. E. "Brief Observations on the Shroud of Turin," *BTB* 14 (1984) 145-148

2112 Bulst, W. "Turiner Grabtuch und Exegese heute," *BZ* 28 (1984) 22-42.

2113 Wild, R. A. "The Shroud of Turin: Probably the Work of a 14th-Century Artist of Forger," *BAR* 10 (1984) 30-46

2114 Bulst, W. "Zur geographischen Herkunft des Turiner Grabtuchs," *BZ* 29 (1985) 104-105.

2115 Heutger, N. "Prokuratoren— Münzen auf dem Turiner Grablinnen," *BZ* 29 (1985) 105-106.

2116 Schnackenburg, R. "Zum Turiner Grabtuch," *BZ* 29 (1985) 103-104.

2117 Bulst, W. "Turiner Grabtuch und Exegese heute II: Neues zur Geschichte des Tuches," *BZ* 30 (1986) 70-91.

2118 Dubarle, A. M. "Le linceul de Turin dans les publications récentes," *EspVie* 96 (1986) 59-64.

2119 Kohlbeck, J. A. and Nitowski, E. L. "New Evidence May Explain Image on Shroud of Turin. Chemical Tests Link Shroud to Jerusalem," *BAR* 12 (1986) 18-29.

2120 Mourlon Beernaert, P. "The Enigma of the Turin Shroud. A Sign, not a Proof," *LumVit* 42 (1987) 34-47.

XXXI. The Passion of Jesus and Noncanonical Works

The Acts of Pilate

2121 Mommsen, T. "Die Pilatus-Akten," *ZNW* 3 (1902) 198-205.

2122 Dobschütz, E. von. "Der Prozess Jesu nach den Akten Pilati," *ZNW* 3 (1902) 89-114.

2123 Winter, P. "A Letter from Pontius Pilate," *NovT* (1964) 37-43.

2124 Lampe, G. W. H. "The Trial of Jesus in the *Acta Pilati*," *Jesus and the Politics of His Day*. Ed. E. Bammel and C. F. D. Moule. Cambridge: 1984, 173-182.

The Gospel of Peter

2125 Vaganay, L. *L'évangile de Pierre*. Paris: 1930.

2126 Denker, J. *Die theologiegeschichtliche Stellung des Petrusevangeliums*. Europäische Hochschulschriften 23. Bern/Frankfurt: 1975.

2127 Fuchs, A. *Das Petrusevangelium*. SNTU B/2. Linz: 1978. (concordance and bibliography)

2128 Crossan, J. D. *The Cross that Spoke: The Origins of the Passion and Resurrection Narratives*. San Francisco: 1982.

2129 Moulton, J. H. "The 'Gospel of Peter' and the Four," *ExpT* 4 (1892-93) 299-300.

2130 Bennett, E. N. "The Gospel According to Peter," *The Classical Review* 7 (1893) 40-42.

2131 Bruston, C. "De quelques passages obscurs de l'Évangile de Pierre," *Revue de théologie et des questions religieuses* 2 (1893) 371-380.

2132 Chapuis, P. "L'Évangile et l'Apocalypse de Pierre I," *RTP* 26 (1893) 338-355.

2133 Funk, X. "Fragmente des Evangeliums und der Apokalypse des Petrus," *TQ* 75 (1893) 255-288.

2134 Hall, I. H. "The Newly Discovered Apocryphal Gospel of Peter," *The Biblical World* 1 (1893) 88-98.

2135 Harris, J. R. "The Structure of the Gospel of Peter," *The Contemporary Review* 64 (1893) 212-236.

2136 Hilgenfield, A. "Das Petrus-Evangelium über Leiden und Auferstehung Jesu," *ZWT* 36/1 (1893) 439-454; 36/2 (1893) 220-267.

2137 Soden, H. "Das Petrusevangelium und die kanonischen Evangelien," *ZTK* 3 (1893) 52-92.

2138 Zahn, T. "Das Evangelium des Petrus," *Neue Kirchliche Zeitschrift* 4 (1893) 143-218.

2139 Barnes, W. E. "The Newly-found Gospel in its Relation to the Four," *ExpT* 5 (1893-94) 61-64.

2140 MacPherson, J. "The Gospel of Peter," *ExpT* 5 (1893-94) 556-561.

2141 Semeria, J. B. "L'évangile de Pierre," *RB* 3 (1894) 522-560.

2142 Koch, E. "Das Petrusevangelium und unsre kanonischen Evangelien," *Kirchlichen Monatschrift* 15 (1895-96) 311-338.

2143 Stanton, V. H. "The 'Gospel of Peter,' " *JTS* 2 (1900) 1-25.

2144 Stocks, H. "Zum Petrusevangelium," *NKZ* (1902) 276-314; 14 (1903) 511-542.

2145 Dibelius, M. "Die altestamentlichen Motive in der Leidensgeschichte des Petrus— und Johannes— Evangeliums," *Beihefte zur Zeitschrift für die alttestamentliche Wissenschaft* 33 (1918) 125-150. = *Botschaft und Geschichte. I: Zur Evangelienforschung.* Tübingen: 1953, 221-247.

2146 Turner, C. H. "The Gospel of Peter," *JTS* 14 (1913) 161-195.

2147 Gardner-Smith, P. "The Gospel of Peter," *JTS* 27 (1925-26) 255-271.

2148 Gardner-Smith, P. "The Date of the Gospel of Peter," *JTS* 27 (1925-26) 401-407.

2149 Perler, O. "L'Évangile de Pierre et Méliton de Sardes," *RB* 71 (1964) 584-590.

2150 Koester, H. "Apocryphal and Canonical Gospels," *HTR* 73 (1980) 105-130.

2151 McCant, J.W. "The Gospel of Peter: Docetism Reconsidered," *NTS* 30 (1984) 258-273.

2152 Wright, D. F. "Apologetic and Apocalyptic: The Miraculous in the *Gospel of Peter*," *Gospel Perspectives VI*. Ed. 401-418.

2153 Crossan, J. D. "The Cross that Spoke," *Forum* 3 (1987) 3-22.

2154 Green, J. B. "The Gospel of Peter: Source for a Pre-Canonical Passion Narrative?" *ZNW* 78 (1987) 293-301.

Index